ADVANCE I

M000207698

"With courage, candor and clini[...] the brave age of sixty-one, under t[...] in EMDR, embarked on a grueling journey; a journey through, and out of, a world of repressed wounds from childhood trauma. Here we meet her multiple adult personalities, her hiding, wounded children and witness the power of the human spirit to rise above pain. She has documented the astonishing ability of the human mind to bury trauma in a grave of unconsciousness, and yet still attain to greater than normal performance and notable accomplishments in life. It is an arresting testimony to the tragic outcome of neglected and damaged children. Whatever happens to children affects them for a lifetime. Thanks to such a tenacious, transparent and tender author, we are all afforded the high hope that healing is possible, no matter the depth of the hidden wounds. A highly recommended read for therapists, concerned family and patients alike."

—ALICE SCOTT-FERGUSON, Therapist and Author

"Janyne McConnaughey bravely becomes the voice for children who have experienced attachment wounding and trauma. I highly recommend this book for all professionals who work with children and adults that struggle with attachment and the far reaching effects of childhood trauma. Not only does her book provide insight into the painful experience of trauma but it helps the reader understand the 'why' behind the behavior of a hurting child. Janyne also boldly speaks hope, which is so desperately needed by those impacted by trauma and the hurt of disrupted attachment."

—HEATHER C. THOMPSON, MS, LPC, Child and Family Therapist

"Dr. Janyne provides a rare glimpse into the world of mental illness. Her insights into the healing process are profound and articulate. The way she painstakingly honors herself in the telling of the story allows the reader to respect her as both the subject matter and the narrator (teacher) who explains a very difficult experience to understand. Truly an inspiration, this story of the successful journey from broken and dissociative to integrated and fully aware provides an excellent narrative of what it takes to overcome the very real, lasting effects of unprocessed trauma in a child's life. I highly recommend it for the professional and for those who love someone living with mental illness like dissociative disorders."

—KIERSTEN ADKINS, M.A., LPC, Exec. Dir., Pathway To Hope

"Not an easy read, yet impossible to put down, Janyne McConnaughey's personal story captures the heart from the first page, as she courageously unfolds the abuse she experienced from early childhood through her adult years. At the beginning, I found it almost too terrifying to read, but the author and her skilled therapist beckoned me into this story of deep pain and—ultimately—healing and wholeness. It may unwrap a few memories of your own as you turn its pages. The good news is that there is promised healing for all who are brave enough to tread back through their own journey."

–SUSAN ELAINE JENKINS, author, *Scandalon: Running from Shame and Finding God's Scandalous Love*

"Janyne McConnaughey is vulnerable in the kind of way that changes the world! Her story challenges us to face life in all its pain, while finding hope and courage to persist. Janyne wrestles with how to think about God in light of her suffering, and that alone makes this book a gem. I recommend it!"

–THOMAS JAY OORD, author, *The Uncontrolling Love of God*

"As a colleague and friend of Janyne's, I walked through this painful time of discovery and therapy with her shortly after the birth of my first child. Janyne's therapy not only changed her life, but it also profoundly affected me and helped form my parenting practices. I now view the thoughts and memories of a child during early formative years as much more robust than I had thought possible. I highly recommend this book to all parents because trauma may occur to a child in spite of a diligent parent's protective efforts. Parents need to know emotional and psychological help is available today that can heal a child before life-long damage is done. Although tragic, Janyne's story gives parents hope that raising a happy, healthy child is possible when they actively participate in their child's life. From Janyne's story we learn that we need to listen to, believe, protect and love the children in our lives."

–LESLIE R. MIKESELL, Ph.D.

"Janyne McConnaughey rewrites the story controlling her life. With the courage to heal, she uses all the resources at her disposal to overcome helplessness, despair, and brokenness. God's uncontrolling love beckons her forward. The emerging narrative is life, joy and intimacy. McConnaughey's faithful imagination and audacity help her persevere with hope. An inspiring memoir of tenacious mercy."

–LON MARSHALL, Licensed Marriage and Family Therapist

BRAVE

A Personal Story of
Healing Childhood Trauma

Janyne McConnaughey, Ph.D.

CLADACH
Publishing

Published by Cladach Publishing
PO Box 336144 Greeley, CO 80633
http://cladach.com

Cover Photo by Chris Barbalis on Unsplash
Cover Design by Kay McConnaughey

ISBN: 9781945099052
Library of Congress Control Number: 2017961955

Printed in the United States of America

To my mother, who never was truly able to know me, but who tenaciously lived her life in a world without hope for healing from her unnamed trauma.

And to every woman who bravely chooses healing so she can fully know and love her children.

TABLE OF CONTENTS

FOREWORD

Janyne McConnaughey may be the most resilient of the resilient clients I saw during many years of therapy. She is also a storyteller. From infancy to young adult years, she had held inside all the intensity of feelings, shame, helplessness, and meaning that were part of each experience of trauma she endured. To cope, she repressed memories detached from feelings, unknowingly created personas to hold the feelings and trauma experiences, and rose above the pain to live the life she was expected to live. This explains the two selves she describes at each age. One held the trauma experience and the other "rose above."

The story she tells is the cognitive retelling of intense therapy—a tortuous journey that uncovered layers of trauma experience held with all the intensity of feelings and the meaning of the experience. The therapy used was EMDR (Eye Movement Desensitization and Reprocessing), a therapy treatment recognized worldwide, that targets unprocessed memories, body sensations, and the meaning of the trauma experience, which are held in the primitive, limbic brain where the fight-or-flight instinct and the feeling centers are located. When trauma has occurred, the instinctual readiness to protect overrides cognition, so anything resembling an emotionally-repressed experience can trigger an intense reaction that can feel overwhelming, confusing and shameful.

Experiencing herself as brave at each of the ages as she processed was a critical piece of her therapy. Janyne was an exceptionally brave child, young adult, and therapy client.

Between therapy sessions, she wrote volumes as she processed what emerged from each intense therapy session and prepared for the next session. She bravely stayed with therapy when she wanted it to be done, and stayed until she was able to connect understanding and compassion with all of herself.

Interestingly, Janyne's Ph.D. is in education with Early Childhood as her focus. Now, with this background, she is ready to use her own experience to help others. This involves understanding the child's experience of connection to self and others. When initial attachment to significant others in a young child's life is missing, and trauma occurs, this connection is absent. Janyne's story shows a path to integration and wholeness.

Susan M. Kwiecien, Ph.D., LMFT, EMDR II, Retired

INTRODUCTION

"My brokenness is a better bridge for people
than my pretend wholeness ever was."

–Sheila Walsh

The most surprising part of my journey has been the number of people who have quietly said to me, "I was also sexually abused as a child." This is not only true of women. The statistic is generally one in four (some say five). This means, if you gather one-hundred men, women, and children in the room, statistically speaking, twenty to twenty five of them have been the victims of sexual abuse (childhood or otherwise). This is also true in a church gathering of one-hundred people. Yet, we live in fear of mentioning it—or if we do, we sense everyone wishes we hadn't.

If you are aware of childhood trauma in your own life, you may have difficulty reading this book. Please seek professional care. My story is likely to make readers sad; but for those who have never received therapeutic healing for trauma, it may open up unresolved wounds. Then again, it may give you hope for a level of healing you never believed possible. This book is intended to increase awareness about the effects of childhood trauma, but professional help is necessary for healing.[1]

Living above the pain is not all that effective. Clinging to scripture and the grace of God, while helpful, does not reach into

---

1. See Addendum: "Childhood Trauma"

the depths of trauma, which may include PTSD symptoms of anxiety, debilitating self hatred, and shame. The abused spend a lifetime carrying the shame of their abusers as their own. In many cases, forgiveness (considered a spiritual necessity for healing) is only an illusion accomplished by repressing or suppressing pain. Pressure to forgive abusers circumvents the necessary process required for true healing.

I, like many others, lived behind a mask while hiding profound trauma and pain. My open sharing of truth will make some very uncomfortable, because it will try to grab the masks from their concealed faces. I was hiding in plain sight but was never alone in doing so. To some degree, we all wear masks, but the use of masks to hide traumatic pain is not a plan I would suggest. In my case, it was much more than a mask—it was the splitting off of parts of my being in order to live. All strategies to live above the pain will eventually fail. I am willing to tell my story if it can help someone—anyone—to seek help before this happens in damaging, uncontrollable ways. I came so close.

Jesus came to heal the brokenhearted, and this described me perfectly. All of me longed for healing. God had always guided and cared for me, so when prompted to make a therapy appointment, I never looked back. Nothing less than complete healing was ever going to satisfy me. All the other options had been tried and had proven to be imposters. Therapy was a terrifying, desperate choice but turned out to be God's gift of love for all the fractured parts of me.

What you will find in these pages is a very selective retelling of my three-year therapy journey. What has been included is for the purpose of demonstrating the effects of childhood trauma and the necessary processes for healing. It is by no means a "tell all." In a few places, there are minor changes for protection, but everything (even the parts which seem like fanciful children's stories) is based on the processing of my memories—most of which were hidden under cover stories.

The story my mother and I share is important. It is only in sharing truth that we can expect to help the next generation fully understand the lifelong effects of insecure attachment and early childhood sexual abuse. The research documenting the effects of abuse within a young child's brain is mounting every day. The repressed emotional memories stored in my body caused a lifetime struggle with both mental and physical illnesses. It is possible to heal an adult who experienced trauma as a child, but how much better it would have been to have received the care I needed before I reaped so many tragic consequences.

What forgiveness and honor looks like toward my mother is an understanding that something happened to her which prevented her from being the mother God intended her to be. I tried to learn what happened to her as a child, but it will never be known. I was the recipient of her deep brokenness, but this does not discount whom she was created to be—or God's love for her.

The following pages share the effects of both the abuse and my mother's inability to provide emotional support. These effects include physical and emotional pain along with those things I came to incorrectly believe about myself. My complete lack of emotion toward my mother was always part of me, but I never understood why. The deadness inside of me was also inexplicable, but it is now understood as the result of one horrible week when I was three.

You may wonder, as you read, if I have truly healed. Some chapters include the raw processing which was necessary for healing. Thankfully, I am no longer there. To achieve wellness, it was necessary to go to the very core of my being. Healing is a messy, painful process and I have shared my journey with honesty and openness. Some might prefer I only share the results of healing and not the difficult process, but this would conceal the painful results of trauma. While I did not have a spiritual problem, I did wrestle with my understanding of God and evil. Some of this wrestling is included, but my spiritual journey is not the focus of this book. This is a book about the effects of childhood trauma.

My hope is for others to understand the psychological trauma incurred by early childhood abuse. The effects are not limited to childhood, and even those who appear to live above it, as I did, reap a life of inner anguish. The remainder of my life will be spent helping others to understand the importance of the mother-child bond and the effects of insecure attachment, which often causes the child to be susceptible to sexual abuse.

My father did his very best to care for his children and the wife he loved. My mother was unable to provide the emotional care I needed. I believe she was as dead inside as she caused me to be. She could have made different choices. I did my best to break the generational pattern while raising my own children. I am not sure this would have been possible for her in the cultural context in which she lived. I wish this were not true. I wish this story were very different. It isn't.

The most important gift my mother gave me was tenacity. We were both "take the tiger by the tail" women. I took this gift and found the answers for which my entire being longed. Some believe it is possible to heal past generations through our own healing efforts. If that is true, then this book is my best effort at healing the wounds of my family. Each of us deserves honor for the lives we lived. Now it is time for me to share my story. I was brave and broken and now I am breathing. I am writing my own ending to my life as I embrace my wholeness and encourage others to be emotionally present for the children in their lives and if necessary to follow their own path to healing.

PART I
BRAVE

There is freedom waiting for you,
On the breezes of the sky,
And you ask, 'What if I fall?'
Oh, but my darling,
What if you fly?

–Erin Hanson, *The Poetic Underground*

What if I fly? My daughter gave me a necklace inscribed with these words. It reminds me of every single fearful day I dreamed of freedom and believed that one day it would be possible to fly.

This is my story. It's about a small girl who was born to love life and live. It's about the terrible and sad things that happened to her but never took away her dream of flying. She always believed she would get on her bicycle and fly over the rainbow to the place where her troubles would melt like lemon drops. This is the story of how I helped her heal so she could fly.

The bravery in the following pages astounds me. I didn't always feel brave. Sometimes, on the way home from therapy, I would sing the song "Brave"[1] to remind myself that my tears were healing me so I could find a way out of the cage in which I had lived my life. If I would ever fly free, I'd have to be brave— and then I would, as the lyrics say, "let my words fall out" so I could help others out of the cages where they lived.

During the fall of 2014, while beginning my thirty-third year as a college faculty member, I sensed it was to be my last year. Retiring was not in my thoughts, but the positions I held were no longer a good fit. At the top of my career, I had achieved a level of respect and was in better shape physically than any other time in my adult life. No; retirement was simply not on the list—it made no sense. I had applied for several other positions at major Christian universities, made it to the final rounds in every case, and was confident a new opportunity would surface.

Then my world turned upside down. The story of being prompted to go to therapy—and what I learned there—is for other chapters. I can tell you this, I had repressed a lifetime of trauma and was quickly coming apart—a fact I unconsciously knew but could not consciously admit. Unbeknown to all who worked with me, during that final year before retirement I completed months of intensive therapy. When another position did not materialize, I retired—only to realize my journey of healing was not yet over. Another year of intensive therapy and healing brought me to a place of wholeness I could have never imagined. The story you find in these pages was tightly held in the deepest part of me...

In the fall of 2016, I enrolled in an online writing course hosted by author, Jeff Brown. I had written hundreds and hundreds of pages while processing the therapy; but Jeff and this course, along with the amazing writers who encouraged me on my journey, allowed me the freedom to find my voice and begin this book. Therapy paused during the class, and I slowly began to stand on my own. The following section was written for the course during this time period, which was a time of great uncertainty in my life. I share it as a snapshot of my life, the place God gave me to heal, and the point of wholeness and continuing healing from which this book was written. What you will read in subsequent chapters will leave you wondering if healing could ever be possible—the answer is yes, but it is a long and difficult process.

---

1. Author's Note: This is an example of how literature and music were interwoven throughout my story and journey of healing. As a child, I wove literature into my fantasies in order to live above the trauma I experienced. The song, "Over the Rainbow," along with other nuances from *The Wizard of Oz* (both the 1939 film and the book by L. Frank Baum, originally published in 1900) will be evident throughout this book. You will also come across *Alice's Adventures in Wonderland*, written by English mathematician Charles Lutwidge Dodgson under the pseudonym Lewis Carroll, and first published in 1865 (from which all quotes attributed to "Alice" throughout this book are taken); and *Pilgrim's Progress*, an allegory written in 1678 by John Bunyan (quotes from which appear throughout this book also). During my thirty plus years of teaching Children's Literature courses, I often wondered about the widely varied emotions elicited by the books of my childhood. I am still discovering these connections. Music was also an important part of my healing. The song, "Brave," sung by Sara Bareillis (written by Bareilles and Jack Antonoff) along with several other popular songs, served as a way to ground myself during many dysfunctional periods of therapy. Where necessary, I have attempted to give credits without disrupting the sense of story. I am forever grateful for all artists, past and present, who have used their creative talents to enrich our lives and give us hope. It is my desire that this, sometimes fanciful, retelling of my healing journey will continue this tradition and give hope to many.

1
From The End of the Journey

COME WALK WITH ME (FALL 2016)

Let me show you my life. Sometimes I have to remind myself this is my life, because it is so different from anywhere I ever thought I would be.

Here my husband and I make our home—in a 32-foot, fifth-wheel trailer. See it there under the trees, which are dropping copious amounts of leaves on our patio area? Inside is cozy and simple—just like my life. Walk with me through the Garden of the Gods RV Resort, and see the now covered pool where my granddaughter learned to swim when she and her brother spent two weeks in our very small home. Then, see the trail that hugs the flowing creek. We will walk by the activity building now closed for the winter, but the dinner bell reminds me spring will return and hopefully, so will the BBQ guy. Someone has a campfire going, and I am glad it is masking the scent on the breeze from the nearby stable. While you are enjoying the view of Pikes Peak, I will stop to show you my tree. It was dead but still grew. New life sprang from the dead hollow trunk and formed a perfectly healthy tree. It is a picture of my transformation, and I always stop and ponder my healing journey and its likeness to this miracle tree.

Maybe we will go to lunch at my favorite restaurant. You should feel honored, because I don't share this place with everyone. It is a protected place of treasured moments and friendships.

I used to be a very public person—no longer. My life used to be full of constant moving and accomplishing—no longer. Quiet and solitude are now treasured. There is contentment in being a companion to my newly found self but also enjoyment in spending time with the few friends who have helped me along my path to healing.

I will probably take out my phone and show you pictures of my family. First there is Scott, who took care of me during my very darkest days. He is looking for a job before his ends and we are poised to move. I will brag on my daughter who is a remarkable single mother of two of the most wonderful children in the world and how she just began a new position as assistant principal of an elementary school. I will laugh remembering some of the *What in the world?* moments she has called and shared with me. It will remind me of how much I love and miss her. I will shine with pride and show you my son, who looks like me, and his wife, who is strong like me, and their busy, busy life as youth pastors. My heart longs to be near them and spend days walking along the Puget Sound. One day it will happen, one day.

Later, we will sit down at a local coffee shop and talk. You might ask me what my plans are for my future. This is a difficult question since being so newly formed as this person whom I suppressed my entire life. Plus, our life is in limbo because of the job situation, so it is very difficult to build new life patterns. My biggest task since finishing therapy is to learn to ride the emotional waves and care for myself. This is all very new for me and fills my days with challenges, but growth is encouraging. My growth is probably like my tree when it first began to grow from inside the hollow trunk. I am very protective of myself and draw strength from this newly grounded place.

Then, I will probably abruptly stop talking about myself

and ask about you—my true essence is caring. If you trust me, you may tell your own painful story. I will listen and be there for you, and your story will build my desire to write in ways that will encourage others to find their true authentic selves under all the layers of life. Maybe you will read some of my writing—I am getting braver all the time about sharing.

When we go our separate ways, there will be gratitude because our paths crossed. I will feel peaceful about the encounter and glad we shared the time together. Back in my cozy writing spot, I will tell a story about my great life and leaving all but the most important things behind to find my true self. Thoughts about my future as this new person will unfold and cause me to determine in my heart that no matter what the future holds, I must always remember who I was on this peaceful day. No matter what is ahead, I will always hold and care for the selves who survived within me.

Finally Understanding Myself

As I began to share my story with my most-trusted friends, they always had questions. I didn't mind the questions, but toward the end of the second year of therapy, I sensed one day it would be crucial to construct a document that would explain what had transpired. For that purpose I wrote the following condensed interview. Calling the interviewer Ms. Skeptic is a clear indication of my fear of not being believed. A few parts have been updated to better reflect my final understandings, but for the most part the wording from the original "interview" is intact and will provide foundational understanding for the following chapters.

The "Interview" (Spring 2016)

My name is Ms. Skeptic and I am here today to interview Dr.

Janyne McConnaughey about her recent revelations concerning her life with a dissociative disorder. She has accepted this interview in hopes she can help others in understanding the disorder. Now, Dr. McConnaughey, for those who do not know you, will you tell us a little about your life?

Honestly, the life story I always told was of a pretty idyllic 1950s childhood. Much of my story of growing up in a preacher's home and serving in church-related educational ministries, and my now thirty-eight year marriage is included here. On the surface, it was a wonderful life!

You are aware most who say they have DID (Dissociative Identity Disorder) do not have such idyllic descriptions of their lives? Were there signs that others might have noticed in you?

The disorder is mostly hidden and often misdiagnosed. A few things are helpful in understanding this. The first is an understanding of what a dissociative disorder is. In my journey, I began to understand dissociation as more of a spectrum. To some degree, in order to cope, everyone dissociates from reality on occasion—daydreaming for instance—very common and usually healthy.

On the other end of the spectrum is the person who separates into multiple identities to divide up the pain and live life. In this category there are some who have periods of amnesia while various "parts" live life. In my case, "DID NOS," (Dissociative Disorder—Not Otherwise Specified) there was not significant amnesia between my alternate identities or "alters." Thus, I didn't wake up and find clothes in my closet that I didn't remember buying. I did have significant blocked memories (due to repression), but none impaired my ability to function on a day-to-day basis.

So no one could tell?

21

No. After I explain it to my closest family and friends, they often say, "Well, that actually makes sense." But we all have quirky things we do, and this was what everyone assumed.

I must pause at this point to say there are those in the field of psychology who do not believe in the diagnosis of DID. What are your thoughts on this?

(Sigh) This is so damaging for those who are dissociative—especially in one specific way. Dissociation at every level on the spectrum is a coping mechanism and as such is not a systemic mental illness—in other words, no one is born dissociative, it is a result of what happened to him or her. Granted, there may be some predisposed tendencies, such as intelligence and creative cognitive coping skills, but it is always the result of some type of trauma—usually sexual abuse at a very young age. As a coping mechanism for trauma, dissociation can be healed. It is complicated but possible. If a professional does not believe in the validity of the diagnosis, then the answer is usually medication—which may alleviate the symptoms to some degree but never addresses true healing.

In addition, being believed was important to my healing. I knew there were three adults in my head and felt myself shift to them periodically through the day. There was nothing in my story to cause me at sixty one to suddenly create a fantasy such as this—for what? Attention? (Laughter, lots of laughter.) Dissociative disorders are all about hiding—especially at my level of what I call "functional dissociation." When I finally came to my own conclusion about being dissociative, it was absolutely crucial to be believed!

Did you know?

Absolutely not. Did I know something was not right? Yes! Most spend years in therapy before it is correctly diagnosed.

When did you decide to seek therapy? What brought you to this decision?

For some, the idea God audibly told me to go to a specific therapist is probably going to be harder to swallow than the disorder itself, but that is exactly what happened. I described my fear of going to therapy in one of my first blog posts. At sixty one, I was at the top of my professional career, a wife, mother, and grandmother, with many wonderful friends—and absolutely terrified.

Why were you afraid?

Great question. I was unaware of living as multiple identities, but did spend my life running away from a "me" I could neither understand nor tolerate. My life was successfully navigated above the turmoil. I didn't understand what it was, but I knew it had the power to destroy my carefully-constructed life.

How long were you in therapy before you understood what you were dealing with?

This is a very simple question, which involves a very complicated answer. My first session, in hindsight, was an amazing display put on by "Janyne" to prove there was absolutely nothing wrong. I was just trying to decide about signing the contract for the following year, since teaching at the college didn't seem like a good fit for me any longer. In the next couple sessions, it became apparent I had mother issues. This is not uncommon—maybe you do too? (Uncomfortable laughter.)

By the third or fourth session we decided I should work through some of my anxiety issues by going back to my childhood memories with my mother. This was when I had my first introduction to EMDR.

Can you explain EMDR?

Yes, this is always a question. It is a recognized, research-validated therapy treatment in which the client remains aware but is able to go below the surface of cognitively processed events and resolve the underlying emotions connected to the memories stored in the limbic brain. It is done in a variety of ways by bypassing the cognitive part of the brain and allowing the experience, with all of the intensity of the attached emotions, to surface. In my case, this also released repressed memories. If unfamiliar with this recognized type of therapy, it might be good to explore the EMDR International Association website.

Why was EMDR so important to your healing?

My survival was dependent on cognitive coping strategies and few therapeutic interventions would have been successful in getting underneath my defenses. There are some concerns that EMDR causes memories to surface too quickly and may overwhelm dissociative clients who do not have strong processing structures in place. As with any therapy, the keys are skillful use and care for the client. For me, EMDR was the avenue of healing.

Why do you believe this was true?

Many with dissociative disorders spend years in various therapeutic situations without ever obtaining a correct diagnosis. The whole purpose of dissociation is to hide subconsciously repressed or suppressed memories. While EMDR is designed as a way to process memories, in my case it also served as a mechanism to retrieve frozen memories from dissociative states. This doesn't mean it would be effective in this specific way for everyone, since each case is unique.

My simple question of "Which one?" (explained in Chapter 4) early in therapy probably moved my healing at warp speed, since it allowed me to see my inner structures of functioning personas and dissociative states. My ability to see and analyze these dissociative structures was a gift, but I would never have allowed myself to see it outside of EMDR therapy. My structures were too perfect and I was too strong.

How do you know the memories were real?

This question voices a common fear. I was concerned that a therapist would convince me something had happened in my early life, but she never did that. This may occur on occasion with the rare, unethical therapist, and probably is the reason for the myth. It is horrible and prevents many from seeking help. Before the first memory of abuse surfaced, I said, "I don't think we are going to find anything, do you?" My therapist never led me down any path. She simply believed in the truth of the memories that did surface.

But how did you know it was real?

My first memory was when I was probably three. While in the memory, there were neither adult words nor understanding to explain the pain. The truth my body told, and the anguish pouring out of me, could not be manufactured. I have no doubts. Once the memories were processed, the related triggers vanished—proof of the connection between the abuse and the triggers that had plagued me all my life. Many of these triggers are explained in the following pages.

So, you have no doubts about the absolute truth of your memories?

Oh! Thank you for asking this question! Anyone who studies memory knows things may not have happened exactly like you remember them. In my case, there were many false cover memories (flat memories without emotion) to hide the real memories.

In every one of them, I was brave and strong and escaped danger. Most of the time, it was illogical that a child, teen, or young adult could have escaped the situation, but my story convinced me. I never said these false versions of the memories in EMDR—even when I wanted to do so. I was a child and while the memory may not be exact, there is no question but something happened— something involving very traumatic sexual abuse. My body told the story during therapy, triggers made me live the memories my entire life, and once I faced the truth, there was nothing in me to doubt it. In fact, it finally made sense.

Didn't remembering make it worse?

This is exactly what I would have thought, but the process of EMDR takes the power out of the memory by releasing it so it can be understood by the adult self. Integration was not possible until the power was removed from the memory.

What is integration?

The first step to becoming one whole person happened to me the day in therapy when I became aware of the three adults who had been living in separate compartments in my brain. I saw them and they saw each other. One of my therapist friends called it a "perfect three-point landing." Recognition happened again and again as the alters entered my conscious world. I knew them immediately and could describe each of their personalities. So the first step was awareness. Then we had to find out why they had been created or split—always trauma of some kind had occurred. Once the trauma was healed, if they were twins (one who lived and one who held the pain), they could become one or integrate.

Integration only comes through healing—the split remains because of unprocessed pain. Shifting is a survival skill. I could not have held all the pain in one person.

The process sounds very complicated—how long were you in therapy?

I almost hesitate to answer this question. If someone is heading into therapy, he or she often wants to know exactly how long it will take to be helped. That's an unanswerable question. I thought I would be "outta there" in a couple sessions. My denial makes me laugh; but in reality, the time it took me to reach integration was unbelievably short. It is very common for people to say eight to twelve years! That seems realistic! It is complicated. I completed the integration of the three adults in less than six months, but was sometimes in therapy for seven to eight hours in a week. What we did in so short a time was literally impossible! To say it is possible or recommend it to anyone would be irresponsible! I did not know how to do this any other way. We all knew this was true. Once the problem presented itself, I attacked it with a vengeance. It was necessary for me to give up almost everything in my life to heal; and I lived through months of hell—while still working. Most of that period of time is a blur. Without my writing, the memory of the deep processing would be lost.

So, never do what I did! Go slowly. Take time. Take breaks. Stabilize. Then go back. Slower would have been better for me; but I didn't know any other way.

Is it hard for you to go back and read what you wrote during therapy?

Sometimes. Most of the raw processing was accidentally deleted. Those raw documents would probably be difficult to read; I did not have a clear sense of self, probably because of the extent of the trauma which created such a disorganized state. Much of my raw processing was transferred to a version of the story in which my identity was carefully disguised—a method, which distanced me from my own pain. I'm saving the volumes of material related to the psychological process of healing, for a later book. It is a very messy process, but true healing cannot happen unless someone is willing to get messy. Getting messy is something we almost always avoid, probably because we think we are the only ones who ever had such awful thoughts. Part of my sharing my messiness in this book is to tell others it is OK—you are not alone. There is so much fear. We need to help each other feel safe.

Is there anything else you would like your readers to know before they read this book?

It is important to say my parents knew what happened to me at three but made choices based on the era in which they lived. My father loved me, and my mother was incapable of being the mother I needed. They both on separate occasions said I was "difficult" as a child. Yes, I imagine I was. It is also important to know I was born in 1953. What happened to me (multiple times) was unthinkable. As children, we were taught to respect adults and obey them. I had no words to describe what happened, and my perpetrators told me no one would believe me. They were right. Therefore, I used every possible God-given coping mechanism to survive.

It is hard to listen to you and not believe you.

(Laughing.) Yes, I wish I could just sit and talk to anyone who is skeptical. My openness and clear honesty is a gift. I have nothing to gain personally by sharing my story—except to help others.

Thank you for sharing so openly with me today. I do think this interview—and your story that follows—will help others to understand more about dissociation. I wish you the best as you continue to live out your life.

Telling the Story

Coming to terms with the truth of my story and the results of the trauma was a multi-faceted task. This "interview" provides background but in no way describes the emotional duress of realizing I had lived my life as multiple selves.

My therapy began in October 2014 and ended during summer 2017 with very few breaks. During several weeklong periods the second year, I only left my small RV home for therapy. I slowly gained balance.

In this book I describe the painful process of healing for two reasons:

1) To demonstrate the damaging effects of childhood trauma. Children seem resilient, but never underestimate the damage. No one knew what I subconsciously hid in order to live.

2) Even with the severe trauma I experienced, healing is possible. It is hard work for client, therapist, and family; but it is possible. Accessing help early in life is the answer.

Many generational patterns could be broken if help were accessed before the hurting child becomes a parent. Sadly, my story of healing began after college, after raising my family, after I completed my career, and while I was trying to enjoy my grandchildren. I had to get to what seemed like the end of everything in order to begin my life again as a whole, healed person. I began by telling the story from the end, but now it is time to return to the beginning.

2
From the Beginning

If you had asked me three years ago to tell the story of my life, I would have given you a perfect synopsis. I was born into a minister's family, lived a lovely childhood of freedom with lots of friends and adults who cared about me. I moved a lot and made many friends. Then I went to college, where I had to move again, because the entire college moved. I graduated with honors and began a forty-year career in education, which included thirty-three years as a teacher educator at the college level. Along the way, I completed a Ph.D. and excelled in everything. Scott and I married in 1979, and we had two children who are now living successful adult lives. We added a daughter-in-law we love and a grandson and granddaughter whom we adore. Since retiring in 2015, we have lived in an RV resort at the foot of the Rocky Mountains where Scott is now General Manager. It has been a wonderful life. Yes, it has.

The story I would not have been able to tell you is a tragic tale of sexual abuse that began at the age of three. In the story I crafted of the wonderful life, the abuse never happened. But it did. I always sensed that was true. When the story surfaced, I was convinced my parents never knew, but this was not true. In the world in which they lived, with the lack of understanding and therapeutic help, along with the need to present the perfect pastor's family, they probably made the best choices they knew how to make. Then, a series of continuing events set in motion a life of dissociation and repression, which caused deep psycho-logical damage, but also enabled me to live completely above repeated traumas—until the age of sixty one.

While this story is dependent on the repressed memories that surfaced during and after therapy, pieces of those memories were always in my conscious mind. There never was a memory which surfaced that was not partially known. I always sensed something had happened: I just couldn't live my life unless the traumatic memories were repressed. The emotional struggle was ever present and pervasive. The battle seemed to be caused by my need to stay above what I believed to be some form of mental illness; but there was nothing genetically or biologically wrong with me. I was born a perfectly normal, healthy, intel-ligent, and engaging baby.

JEANNIE IS BORN

On a sunny day in Albuquerque, New Mexico, one small, five-year-old boy called Dick was being watched as he played at a park. His older brother, Lee, was looking bored and irritated because he had been given this task. He would certainly have rather been playing with his friends—of course he would, he was only eleven. It had been a complicated day for the family. Their father, who was the pastor of a young, growing church, was performing a funeral service for an infant child. At the same exact time, their mother had been admitted to the hospital to give birth to her third child, Janyne Ann Jenkins—Jeannie.

As was the custom of the day, the mother was sedated during delivery, and the baby was taken to the nursery where she remained during the five-day recovery period. Exhausted from her busy life, the mother took full advantage of this time to rest. By her own admission, she seldom saw little Jeannie.

Jeannie arrived home a healthy eight-pound baby with blue

eyes and scarcely any hair. She was the apple of her father's eye; but he and her mother were very busy. They often left her in the care of her oldest brother, who found her interesting but was irritated by this responsibility—though he cared about Jeannie always.

Full of life, Jeannie soon got moving, with one curl of hair on her head. From pictures, it appears that she was always ready to smile and engage the world. There was just one problem— engaging just didn't work with her mother, who never looked directly into Jeannie's eyes. She adjusted to this because she had her brother and, when her father came home, he doted on her. She would be a daddy's girl until he died at one hundred, just two days before her sixty-third birthday.

Jeannie's other brother, Dick (later Rich or Richard), was a busy boy and could be counted on to climb everything in sight (there are pictures to prove this)! He was not happy to share the attention with this new child who seemed to charm the world. That would be a problem, because there just wasn't enough attention to go around.

(On the surface this description sounds healthy. However, it doesn't fully portray my underlying attachment issues. After turning forty, I went back to Albuquerque and talked with a family friend who babysat me as a small child. She said, "If you ever got any nurturing, it was from your dad. Your mother probably should not have had children—but then we wouldn't have you and your brothers." This was the only person I ever considered my mother's friend. She knew my mother had accomplished many remarkable things, but being a nurturing mother simply wasn't one of them.)

JEANNIE GROWS UP

Born in 1953, my early life was enveloped by simple

childhood pleasures and memories. The church was my second home, filled with friends from our first days in the nursery. I was my busy father's constant companion. I remember trying to keep up with his long-legged loping gate.

One day I was in his office and asked for a rubber band, which he handed to me.

"No," I said, "not that. A rubber band!"

"Jeannie, this is a rubber band."

Holding up my finger, I said, "But I have an 'owie.' That isn't what I need, I need a rubber band."

"Oh! A Band Aid!"

It would be many years before I could keep those two words straight, and we would always share laughter. We had the same laugh.

My oldest brother was my other favorite companion. Standing at the screen door, I watched and always wanted him to take me with him, as he left to spend time with his friends. One day he came home with a motorbike.

"Take me on it!" I cried.

He did—two times around the driveway. I could not have been happier!

In front of my house grew a row of beautiful flowers. The Iris became my favorite flower for my entire life. Sandia Mountain stood tall above the flat landscape of Albuquerque, a constant part of my childhood. Sandia was also the name of the church, and much later my dad would find out the name meant "watermelon." He laughed and said, "I wouldn't have called the church Sandia if I had known what it meant."

I can still hear his laughter.

It was such a normal childhood, except for knowing my mother didn't love me. One time, after seeing other children on their mothers' laps, I climbed onto my mother's lap to put my head on her shoulder, but it felt awkward. There were enjoyable memories connected to my mother—her sparkling broaches (which glittered in the sun and created rainbows all around) and playing with the buttons in the button box (which smelled like cedar). I saved the cedar box and broaches as mementos of quiet enjoyment while near my mother. The cross necklace I begged to look into constantly to read the Lord's Prayer—so tiny and magnified—is gone because my mother "didn't know I liked it."

LEARNING TO BE BRAVE

I have many wonderful memories of my father. One day, while at the top step of the stairs to the attic, my father stood below me instructing me how to carefully get on the landing and then turn and crawl backwards down the steps. I was small, maybe three. After my constant begging to go up into the room inside the steeple, he knew one day I would find the door unlocked and go up by myself. He knew this because it was just who I was.

I stood looking down at my father.

"Be brave, Jeannie," he said.

There was an edge without a railing, and I had a healthy fear of heights; but he was there carefully guiding me. He was teaching me to take care of myself.

The stairway was not the only time he asked me to be brave. On another day, I could not stop crying and my mother was in distress. Something very bad had happened to me, and she was unable to stay in the room. My father said, "Jeannie, I need you to be brave. I need to go help your mother."

It was a lot to ask of a small child; but from somewhere deep inside me, I can still feel myself gather up strength in order to be brave for my father. We never talked about that day, but I always sensed him asking me to be brave.

Just before my sixty-third birthday, while on a trip to Indiana, the nurse called to tell me my father had passed. He had chosen full-body donation and would be gone by the time we could catch a plane and get back home to Colorado. The dreaded words rang in my ears as I got out of the car and ran across a park.

"I wasn't there! I wasn't there! He died and I wasn't there!"

Many days I *had been* there. We had celebrated his 100th birthday. We were there every day for the four years he had lived with us. But we weren't there on *this* day. We told him we would be back in four days. But he left when I wasn't there.

A group of firefighters taking a break at the park stopped to watch me. This was oddly comforting and embarrassing all at the same time. It was important to keep breathing.

Then the memory of my father's voice came to me, "Be brave, Jeannie. Be brave."

He had been proud of my life. He always counted on me to be brave.

There was no way to tell my father I had repressed the memory of that tragic day (along with many other soul-wrenching memories). My life was one of someone who appeared to have never experienced trauma. The pain didn't explode from my fractured soul until after age sixty. While processing ever-surfacing painful memories, during week after week and month after month of therapy sessions, this small self had gathered strength to be brave. My father left this world never fully understanding how brave his daughter had truly been, but he was proud anyway.

Now as I take the first step down the scary attic stairway—no longer backwards as a small child, but with the confidence of a woman who was brave enough to find her true self under layers of protection, my father is no longer here to catch me. Still, as I begin to tell my story, my soul can hear my father's voice.

"Be brave, Jeannie. Be brave."

KEEPING THE STORY LINEAR

In storytelling style, this chapter has taken you from my birth to the more recent experience of my father's death. It is the background you will need to follow my journey through therapy on the following pages. Much of this book is composed of processing pieces. As I read it over, I often feel the gaps in the storyline but am hesitant to "fix" all the disconnects since they provide a window into both the processing and the often-disjointed ways in which my story emerged.

My therapy journey often took me in fast-forward and backwards circles. The truths about my life never surfaced as one whole picture. Often, as in the case of the three-year old, the complete story surfaced in multiple, fractured pieces over several months and years. Pieces of the story could only surface and be understood as the accompanying pain could be processed.

To keep it linear, I have attempted to uncoil the story. To do this, I need to take you past growing up, past college, past graduation and first jobs, past marrying and raising two children, and past forty years working in the field of education. This will take you to the year of my sixty-first birthday. Life was really perfectly perfect in every way except one. My soul was coming apart.

> *The White Rabbit put on his spectacles. 'Where shall I begin, please your Majesty?' he asked.*
> *'Begin at the beginning,' the King said gravely, 'and go on till you come to the end: then stop.'*
>
> —Alice

3
I Went to Therapy

"Healing may not be so much about getting better, as about letting go of everything that isn't you—all of the expectations, all of the beliefs—and becoming who you are."

–Rachel Naomi Remen

What is healing? If you break your arm, healing takes place when your bones knit back together. If you fall and gash your leg, healing takes place when new skin replaces the damaged skin. If your heart needs repair, a surgeon can go in and fix it.

What about healing psychologically? It would be so simple if you could just take your brain in and leave it for a few days while a therapist "fixed" it. Instead, a therapist can only be a guide to your healing. Add to this complexity the fact that you may be completely unaware of what it is you are trying to heal—but you are the only one who can find the truth—and your brain may be doing everything in its power to never let you or anyone else see the problem. It is definitely messy.

It is a bit disconcerting to remember how messy things had to get before I could begin to heal. It is also a bit disconcerting to let the world inside to see the messiness. The bright side is, if I could come out on the other side, then healing is possible! But in order for that to happen, I had to go to therapy.

SITTING ON THE COUCH

I sat on the therapist's couch telling my story and showed pictures of my family, friends, and all the places I had just visited.

Yes, my mother and I never had a relationship; but other than a tragic sequence of events as a young adult, it had truly been a wonderful life.

Well, then there were all the times the church, which fed and clothed me, turned against me. But that was history.

My childhood was a typical 1950s and 60s story. My father was a preacher, my mother a teacher, and the good people in the church loved me.

Beginning when I was ten, we moved a lot and it was difficult for me, but it helped me learn to make friends.

"Janyne, you mentioned in our first phone conversation that your mother lived until she was ninety four, and she wore you out. Can you tell me more about that?"

The memory of the phone conversation—and how I had blurted this out about my mother—was still a bit embarrassing. Since being perfect was my main objective, I wasn't convinced I wanted to talk about it; but something about this white-haired, petite, gentle woman made me feel safe.

She waited.

My attempts to distract myself from the stress building inside me were proving unsuccessful. For a moment her name distracted me. Dr. Susan Kwiecien—an unusual name. She waited. I would just call her Dr. Sue. She was maybe my brother's age. We both had a Ph.D. behind our names. We'd probably have interesting conversations outside of this room.

She waited.

MY WORDS WERE CAREFULLY CHOSEN

"Well, she had some mental health issues. There wasn't really any help for her. She would get paranoid and we would have to move. She mostly raised me by bribing—but never kept up her end of the bargain. She was never abusive. She was just not made for nurturing. We never connected."

It felt silly. Why was I in therapy with mother issues? It was embarrassing. I had overcome it, right? Yet, I knew the truth. My mother had been dead for five years and still haunted me. If honest, the results of insecure attachment had been obvious to me since studying child development in college. Yes, I had mother issues. There were many ways this had affected me, but I kept those effects carefully hidden. Maybe we could get to it with the type of therapy she used. Maybe there was a way to be free of the effects.... (If it had only been so easily accomplished!)

Dr. Sue had explained the therapy we would eventually be doing. I didn't really think there would be much that would surface. I wasn't overly concerned as she explained.

"Part of the therapy you will be doing is called EMDR. It stands for Eye Movement Desensitization and Reprocessing. It allows you to get behind your cognitive thinking to access emotional experiences and repressed memories stored in the limbic brain. It is a type of therapy supported by extensive research and will help you to take the power out of disturbing memories."

There *were* painful memories, so this sounded like a positive path. Maybe this was the answer. I knew I had mother issues—not severe, just sad. If possible, I'd like to leave those behind.

WHAT I NEVER EXPECTED

After two more sessions of my incessant and avoidant talking, I chose a simple, uncomplicated memory to process with EMDR. Dr. Sue explained we would sit knee-to-knee with my hands on my knees and she would use an EMDR tapping method on the tops of my hands. My eyes would be closed.

In the memory I chose to process, my mother had bribed me to let her cut my hair. I loved how my ponytail swished when I ran, but she promised me a doll I really wanted....

I am sitting on the bed crying.[1]

(I began sobbing and shaking, but Dr. Sue's gentle voice calmed me as I felt myself delve into the memory in a way I had never before experienced.)

I let her cut my hair, and she is going to break her promise. I am smarter than this. She always breaks her promises. Why did I trust her? I put bobby pins in my short hair and hide it under a cap. It is hot outside but I don't want anyone to see. On the playground my teacher asks me why I have a cap on. I am crying. "Let me see." I feel her remove a bobby pin. "Oh look how it curls and shines in the sun! Everyone will think it is beautiful. Let's take out all the pins." I feel so grateful for her kindness and touch.

Suddenly, a new memory ...

I am on a bed in our den, kicking. My grandfather is tickling me. I kick hard and hear a crack. My kicking has broken his pocket watch. They are all mad at me, because I broke the watch. It is a special watch. I broke the glass. They could have replaced the glass but they didn't. They just kept blaming me for breaking the watch. I didn't want him to tickle me. I told him to stop!

---

1. Author's Note: As EMDR became a part of therapy, I would often continue processing between sessions in ways similar to what I had experienced during the session. I began writing about this processing in story-like ways. Both EMDR retellings and the processing are italicized here, but the context of "in therapy" or "as part of processing" should be clear. My ability to "take therapy home" was an essential part of the progress I made in so short a time.

The hot wash of shame swept over me as Dr. Sue began to gently reassure me that it wasn't my fault. They should have fixed the watch. I was trying to take care of myself.

My eyes were still closed as I processed the memory. I had asked him to stop. I never liked being tickled.

After a few moments, Dr. Sue asked me to come back to my adult self.

"Which one?"

My eyes flew open and the room began to spin around me.

"Is there more than one?" she asked.

"Yes, there are two, maybe three. No, there are three." With that pronouncement, it felt as if Alice had landed with a thud on the floor of the rabbit hole in her head.

Dr. Sue and I talked about the memory we had just processed. I was grateful she was moving on, because the room needed to stop spinning. She returned, though, to what I had said about the three adults, and asked me if it still felt true.

"Yes, I know who they are. I can go home and describe them and come back with descriptions."

Walking out in a fog, I got to the security of my car and began driving. Calling my husband, I said, "Scott, this was way more than I expected."

"Why?" he asked.

"I told her there were three of me." My calm voice belied the distress I had felt during the session. The words echoed in the car and hung in the air for a few seconds before he said, "OK, that makes sense. Do you need me to come get you?"

"No, just don't hang up. I need to keep talking to you until I get there."

How Could This Happen?

Nothing in my life prepared me for what I had just said. I

honestly felt fine. I looked great, had lost one-hundred pounds, was in prime shape for sixty one. When it was clear God was prompting me to go to therapy—to a specific therapist—it made sense for it to only be about the struggle to sign my contract for the following year. Now, over two years later, Dr. Sue and I often stop to remember those early therapy sessions.

"Dr. Sue, remember when I walked into your office the first time?" We laugh. We always laugh about how perfect I appeared and how I insisted I just needed a couple sessions to clarify my life goals.

"I just need to answer the question about signing the contract, and I will be out of here." It was denial. Dr. Sue always answers this playful give and take with a smile.... "No, it won't take us very long."

In the midst of our laughter, we usually pause to look at each other with the knowing look of how absolutely miraculous it was that I came … and trusted. We reflect on how hard I fought to heal the layers, which should have kept me in therapy for ten years, if not my entire life. We know I am a walking miracle and always have been.

The day I said, "Which one?" launched us on an unforgettable journey. Dr. Sue was the therapist: I was the client. But together, we were a team. My healing is a tribute to my tenacious determination and to her unflinching belief that I could be healed. She trusted me and I trusted her; and when I wasn't drowning in pain, our laughter brought peace into my chaos. She is ever-present in this story because of her complete dedication to my healing process.

No, this was certainly not about signing a contract. It was about a repressed story so filled with trauma it caused me to live with a fractured mind my entire life. Again and again, I would ask, "Dr. Sue, do you believe I can be rewired?"

The answer was always yes.

4
The Three Chairs

"I had three chairs in my house: one for solitude, two for friendship, three for society."

–Henry David Thoreau

I t would be impossible to explain the surreal feeling of discovering I was living life as multiple personas. It is kind of like thinking you are a tree and waking up to find out you are a car. I know, that illustration is random; but so is walking into therapy as one person and walking out as three. The most frightening part was it made complete sense to me—and to my husband. Everything in me wanted him to say it didn't make sense, but that would have just made things worse. It absolutely did make sense.

The following day, unable to go to my office, I sat on the floor in a corner of my basement and began making chart after chart of my new understanding of my inner reality. My three personas were sitting in metal chairs (implements of torture to which my back had been subjected for years). They sat in a triangle looking intently at one another. I wrote:

Slowly the fog of sleep lifted revealing the three metal chairs—cold, gray, unforgiving. Like three points of a triangle they stood in stark contrast to the emptiness around them. Three shadows formed from the void, taking their places in the unforgiving chairs. Three chairs, three shadows, three voices.

I had clearly fallen down Alice's rabbit hole.

Sorting It All Out

When I used to read fairy tales,
I fancied that kind of thing never happened,
and now here I am in the middle of one!
                                              –Alice

As a Children's Literature instructor, I was familiar with the story of *Alice in Wonderland*. Fantasy was my favorite genre. I enjoyed imagining myself part of impossible, implausible adventures; but now, like Alice, I had fallen down a rabbit hole, and I wondered what was to become of me.

Descriptions of the three, whom I had plainly seen during the previous session, began to fill yellow notepads. After teaching psychology for years, I was aware the descriptions looked oddly like what was now called DID (Dissociative Identity Disorder). It was slightly comforting to think that didn't really fit me. I didn't wake up to find clothes in my closet I didn't remember buying—though I would have enjoyed that. There certainly were no holes in my memory, nor did people tell me I had done things I couldn't remember—in fact my memory was almost too exacting. This was comforting, kind of like Alice pinching herself at the bottom of the rabbit hole to make sure she was awake and still herself. I was still myself.

Yes, I was still Janyne, but it was clear that at various moments of the day, I was only one part of me. There was Janyne—the one I liked to think of as being the true me—fun loving, free spirited, always living on the edge of decorum. Then, there was the taskmaster, whom I was now calling Non Janyne. She was a consummate professional, all business, and could produce more in a day than seemed humanly possible. She had been given honors and awards and had been responsible for controlling every move

I made in order to lose one-hundred pounds. Last on the list was Jane. She was named Jane because I hated when people mispronounced my name. She was the emotional one—pathetic, really. She made me cry in faculty meetings and dragged me into horrible debilitating depressions, which I called the dark cloud.

Yes, I could describe these three! I returned to the next session very proud of my work.

Killing Jane

Back on the therapy couch, feeling somewhat uncomfortable but desperate for help, my eyes stared at Dr. Sue as she asked me to tell her what I was feeling.

I pulled out my yellow notepad, which would be a constant companion for many sessions. Laughing, I said, "There are three of me." I described them.

It was clear this woman was truly curious about what had been written on the notepad. I sensed the great possibility of going down in the books as one of her most fascinating clients. This was not a comfortable possibility, and I wasn't sure why I trusted her.

While showing her the charts, I provided glowing descriptions of Janyne and Non Janyne. Then moving on to troublesome Jane, I explained how she was a constant emotional mess and threatened to destroy my life.

"You don't have much use for Jane, do you?"

What? "No! I am here to get rid of her."

"She holds your feelings," Dr. Sue observed in the quiet unassuming way that would always tip me over.

Feeling the familiar spot of nonresponsiveness that had always confused me, I stared at my shifting corner looking for someone to come up with a clever answer to the observation. The silence in the room was deafening. Apparently no one was going to help me out, so I turned and looked at Dr. Sue for a long time.

"Yes, she does hold my feelings, and that is why I need to get rid of her. Yes, get rid of her is exactly what needs to be done."

I remained adamant for the remainder of the session but promised to try to rethink my position before returning. I had no plan to embrace Jane or my feelings. But I was willing to rethink getting rid of her.

During that restless night I dreamed about calling Christina Yang from *Grey's Anatomy* and asking her to come over and cut Jane into pieces so I could put her in a plastic bag and throw her over a cliff. Christina agreed. I felt very good about the outcome of the rather gruesome dream.

Back on the couch, Dr. Sue looked at me quizzically and asked, "Have you rethought your desire to be rid of Jane?"

I explained the dream. We laughed; but it was clear we had work to do.

"I did think of one thing Jane helps me with," I admitted.

"What is that?" Dr. Sue looked both pleased and relieved.

"She holds empathy. She steps in when I talk to my college students who are going through a rough time. She has a hard time not crying with them. She makes them feel better about their situations."

She smiled.

I was proud. It was a start. We were on our way to healing Jane, but it was going to be a long journey, because she held all the pain. Despite this glimmer of hope, I would return to the next session with additional documentation for the need to rid myself of Jane.

Who Needs Feelings?

"You are still very negative about Jane," Dr. Sue said.

"Well yes, she is needy. She is clingy. She is emotional. She gets in the way. We don't need her."

As the uncomfortable emotions began to surface, we continued to process the feelings which I was still clearly rejecting. After Dr. Sue helped me make the connection between my rejection of Jane and my feelings, I began to consider the situation.

"Yes, I suppose rejecting feelings is what it is. Maybe that is why there is a 'do not enter' sign under the wife role on my chart."

"What does that mean?"

"Jane, the needy emotional side, would have ruined our marriage. I would have been jealous, paranoid, needy—it would have ruined us. We would have been divorced in a matter of a few years. Jane couldn't be there."

We began processing my awareness of what I was actually saying about Jane (whom I was beginning to accept as a part of my being) and the possibility there might be merit in her feelings. Despite new levels of awareness, I was still sure there was not any value to Jane. I was in absolute fear of my feelings. Jane was the one who embarrassed me by crying in interviews and meetings. She was the one who relived pain again and again. She was the one who fell into depression. She was the needy one. And she simply was not needed.

I had this figured out and was OK with it. Dr. Sue just needed to help me get rid of her. We were certainly clarifying why I felt Jane was a problem but not making much progress in accepting her!

Valuing the Rejected

The sessions continued and as much as I did not want to admit it, Jane did begin to appear to have a role. My descriptions of her began to change, but not until layer after layer was peeled away. All the while, the three adults in my head took turns presenting their viewpoints about the situation in which we had found ourselves.

We were a long way from having them sit together in the three chairs, speaking with one voice, but I did manage to return with a chart listing value for all three. Janyne and Non Janyne just flowed onto the notepad: Jane emerged slowly. She was still not a strong member of the group, but it was possible she might have some minimal value. I was not convinced, but there was relief in the fact the task was complete.

(In hindsight, this chart which was created at some point during the first two months of therapy, is a prime example of my need to process on a cognitive level, but in no way portrays the emotional turmoil involved in getting to a place where these descriptions could be written.)

Janyne:
- Everyone wants to spend time with her
- She brings joy and laughter to the world
- Makes dreams seem possible
- Believes the impossible

Non Janyne:
- Adds wisdom to Janyne
- Provides care and support to bring joy to others
- Orchestrates ways to make laughter happen
- Plans, organizes, takes steps to make dreams come true
- Problem solver in the face of impossible

Jane:
- Empathizes with the pain of others
- Clings to joyful memories to pull me through

- Seeks laughter to reduce pain and stress
- Reminds me that when I push too hard for dreams, structures collapse
- When all emotional support fails, she figures out ways to get needs met

Yes, my opinion of Jane was slowly changing. I began to wonder why she was so damaged. This was a major breakthrough. Was there a possibility it might not be her fault? I wasn't convinced, but my first EMDR session had revealed there were three of me, so maybe there were other factors I did not understand. It was probably necessary to go further.

THREE-CHAIR CONVERSATIONS

At this point, all three adults had formed clear identities, and I had come to believe they all held value. This did not mean they valued each other. They were at war with one another, fighting for the role of host. In a blur of therapy sessions, each of the three took turns at being blamed. At one point, Jane and Janyne vented their anger at Non Janyne's control. Then, Janyne and Non Janyne told Jane she was to blame.

Finally, Jane stood up for herself and made the other two realize she had been holding the pain in silence all those years, and she had been quiet while Janyne "found herself" and enjoyed life. Sometimes Janyne would come to the session only to be pushed aside by Non Janyne. Often Jane would appear unexpectedly with anguishing pain, which filled the room.

All the shifting became confusing. Sometimes Dr. Sue simply asked, "Who has come to the session today?"

Many were the nights when I cried in my sleep. Unable to climb the stairs to go to work, I made excuses, fought through the fog to accomplish the essentials, filled small yellow note pads, and dreamed about throwing one or more of my parts off cliffs. Then I would get up and walk through several days as an apparently normal person—but the conversations in my head were deafening. Triggers sent me back to bed or to the floor again and again and were at first unexpected. As I began to recognize the triggers, there were ways to brace myself to once again drown in a whirlpool.

While working through childhood memories, I felt myself fighting going any deeper, and moved on to the young adult— finally facing significant betrayals and their impact, some of which I had completely minimized up to this point.

After wandering through painful relationships, we discovered the impact of moving and my search for attachment figures. I wrote volumes, talked through the pain, and freed myself from the power of the memories during EMDR therapy. As layers healed, it often brought out new memories, which would then send me into a new unexpected spiral. It was hard to explain the bottomless well of pain exploding from my soul day after day and night after night. Therapy brought temporary relief but also unearthed new layers. The floodgates had been opened, and there was no stopping the deluge.

Calling for help from Dr. Sue or Scott was almost impossible, but eventually I realized getting help could shorten the drowning episodes. I begged Dr. Sue to assure me I would come out on the other side. (She always said, "This is where you are today, but you will not always be here.") The storm was relentless until the night I woke up at one o'clock and found all three of my adult selves sitting in the unforgiving metal chairs.

"What the hell happened here?" they said with one unfiltered voice.

The space between them was a vacuum. There was no anger, no blaming, and most frightening, no purpose.

Still, seeing them all together was somehow comforting, and I fell into a deep sleep.

GATHERING IN THE CHAIRS: MAKING A PLAN

When I woke in the morning, the three were there in the metal chairs, actually talking to each other in unusually calm voices. I grabbed the yellow notepad and began recording their conversation.

> *Janyne was glad to have Non Janyne back. She was having a hard time living life without her—but she didn't want to be controlled. Both Non Janyne and Janyne told Jane they didn't really hate her, but they were afraid she would implode their carefully constructed life. Jane felt betrayed about all they had revealed to Dr. Sue and was still not sure the therapist could be trusted. The other two began to try to convince her, but Jane was simply not OK. Once Non Janyne promised to not control her and Janyne told her she wasn't angry, Jane began to feel more hopeful.*
>
> *The three adults were beginning to work things out in my head. It amused me how the uncomfortable metal chairs irritated them. I tried to replace them, but it never seemed to work. They began to express what they needed. Non Janyne needed a plan. Janyne needed to have some fun. Jane needed to be believed and trusted. Everyone agreed Jane needed to go back and talk to Dr. Sue some more.*

The importance of this day cannot be overemphasized. I had reached the point where the three were no longer at war with each other. They might not fully trust each other, but they were willing to work together to find the answers—answers buried in repressed childhood memories. Integration was the goal, but it could not happen without understanding why I had fractured in the first place.

5
The Reason I Fractured

Most people who did not have a secure attachment with their mothers do not fracture and create alters as I did. There had to be another reason. Sexual abuse as a young child is a likely cause, yet everything in me wanted to deny the possibility. Only a terrifying journey into the depths of my being would enable me to find the truth.

TRUST VS. MISTRUST

The voice came from deep inside of me. *I don't trust you.*

Dr. Sue looked at me quizzically. "You are not trusting me."

She watched me closely as my mind struggled to understand and verbalize my feelings.

In that particular moment, no, I was not trusting her.

Trust was failing, but I knew this was unreasonable in the current circumstance. What was the source of this mistrust? Had I trusted too much and now my trust terrified me? Was there a need not to trust? Every carefully built inner rule designed to protect myself had been broken. Protection was necessary, because I always trusted too much. Every day began with trust even when it made no sense. Even those who had broken my trust were trusted.

While reflecting on this dilemma, it occurred to me that my need to trust was a deep-seated dysfunction. Could trusting be a dysfunction? Apparently in my case, the answer was yes.

The therapy session had begun uneventfully. After talking through some processing from the previous session, Dr. Sue asked, "Do you know where you need to go?"

It would have made sense to go to the age when trust develops—during Erickson's psychosocial stage of trust vs. mistrust in infancy—but in this moment the one who wasn't trusting was an adult. It seemed more logical to go to an adult memory.

Yes, some hurtful things had happened to me as an adult.

"I am in my office, and I just got the letter out of my box. The rest of the department is in another office. I am alone. I feel so alone. I was fired. I have to leave at the end of the semester. I thought they would listen to me. I thought they would let me stay until the other job came through. I thought I had done enough, worked hard enough, proven myself enough to be believed and trusted to stay. I was wrong. They told me I have to leave. I need to leave to go to my grad class. I am crying. I am alone. Then I hear them laughing...."

Laughing. Every time this memory had replayed in my head in the past, it had not included the laughter from the office next door. These were my friends, but the secretary confided they had remained in the office in order to inform the administration of my reaction upon receiving the letter—and they were laughing.

Underneath the shock from their laughter was a profound sense of betrayal of my trust in God to protect me. My belief was that if I were honest, open, and truthful, then God would bless me and protect me. That was not the case.

The pain of hearing the laughter sank in as my eyes opened. Laughter had always been a joyful sound, but now it was a threat. Staring at Dr. Sue, I said, "I don't trust God. To guide me, love me, provide for me, yes; but not to protect me. I don't trust God for that."

I began to question many of the words coming out of my mouth. Was this true? Did I really not trust God to protect me? It was so confusing because my life had been a series of gigantic leaps of faith, which could not have occurred without trusting God. Was it possible to fundamentally trust and not trust at the same time?

Somehow, reaching this memory of my friends' betrayal during my distress, struck an unbelievably deep chord. As if from a distance, I could hear Dr. Sue asking me a question....

"What are you feeling? Is this like your mother?"

Suddenly I was in a movie. Danger was coming. I had to protect myself. I saw the panic button on the wall and lunged for it. Slam, slam, slam, slam—protective doors closed in on every side of me, and I said, "I don't trust you."

Dr. Sue was watching me closely and said, "You are not trusting me."

There was so much involved in this. I did trust, but should I? I had often trusted when I should not. My need to trust warred inside of me with the understanding that no one can really be trusted. God was no different. God had made my life wonderful but never protected me from the pain, which engulfed me from my earliest years. I had lived two lives. In one, lived the "amazing me"—strong, intelligent, accomplished, loving, and free. In the coexistent life, I was damaged, hurting, fearful, needy, and dysfunctional. One trusted; the other did not.

For months I had allowed my dysfunctional life to have a voice, and it was terrifying. If this journey was only for the purpose of self awareness, then I was there. If this journey was only to remove the pain from the haunting memories, then I was there. If this journey was only for the purpose of thinking differently about who I was, that had certainly been accomplished. But there was more. Something was very wrong.

"I'm not done," my voice said through the fog in my head.

"What do you mean?"

"I still need you."

"Yes; but it frustrates you, doesn't it?"

There are no words to express how much it frustrated me. As the session ended, I was more confused than ever—and possibly more frightened. Telling Dr. Sue about the panic room and the one who was screaming there was impossible. It would have been wise to do so, but it was simply too frightening.

My sense of progress was gone, even though there had been a clear difference in my ability to function. Scott could see it—the edge was gone. There was progress, but the stairs suddenly became impossible to climb again.

Calling Dr. Sue's number, I left a message asking for help because there didn't seem to be any other option. It was challenging to try to live a functional life while the dysfunctional life, locked in the soundproof panic room during EMDR, was screaming. She was begging for help, but she frightened me. She was screaming but silenced. There was no way to know why she was screaming, but going there would surely send me into whirlpools again.

CARING FOR JEANNIE

The call came from Dr. Sue, and I sheepishly explained my failure to tell her about the panic room.

"Scott thinks we need to go back and find out why I shut down EMDR and locked myself in the panic room."

It was easier to blame this on Scott, but Dr. Sue and I both understood I needed help. We made a plan to meet the following afternoon.

Life was busy and there was a need to simply move through it—but I was not OK. The only way to live was to keep the panic room tightly closed as the evening's activities ended and my weary body climbed into bed.

Something startled me awake and it frustrated me to see it had only been an hour since falling asleep....

The person, the child, was still in the panic room. It was Jeannie, the small, young version of me. I opened the door, and she motioned for me to follow her down a long hallway at the back of the panic room.

"No Jeannie, we can't go there tonight. We need Dr. Sue to go with us. She is going to take us there tomorrow. We need to wait."

She seemed to accept this and allowed me to fall back asleep—only to wake again and find her beckoning me. This continued for several hours. If anyone was going to get sleep, I would have to figure out how to care for Jeannie.

"Jeannie, can you tell me why you want me to go with you?"

"You need to understand what happened. You need to know what it was like. You need to feel what I felt."

Looking at her sadly, I said, "Yes, I do understand. You need me to go there and this will happen tomorrow, but we both need Dr. Sue to go with us. It would not be good for us to go alone. How can I take care of you tonight?"

Then it struck me. When Jeannie was upset she always needed her little white stuffed puppy. She needed to wipe her tears on his ears. She needed to hold him. I knew where he was.

The grown me said, "Janyne, think about this. Are you really going there? The voices in your head are taking you over the edge. This is a bit irrational."

Yes it was, but the rational line had been left behind long ago, and Jeannie needed the puppy. The puppy was in a box in the closet, which had already supplied other clues. My need to carry such a random collection of things with me for so many years finally made sense. Time and time again I had pulled things from the box on the shelf. The box held breadcrumbs to help me on my journey. It was happening again.

With the puppy retrieved and in my arms, I crawled back in bed praying Scott would not wake. This was just going to be too difficult to explain.

Jeannie held the puppy as she curled up and fell asleep.

PREPARING TO FOLLOW JEANNIE

The three appeared and sat down around the sides of the panic room. They occupied three walls. I sat down on the fourth side. We all decided Jeannie might get cold, so we found a blanket and covered her. She looked so small inside the room, but we knew better than to underestimate her strength. She had a job to do tomorrow and we needed her to rest.

As the four of us began to talk, Non Janyne felt good about this plan for everyone to get some sleep. "You know, she has shown us how to get where we need to go. Tomorrow you, grown up Janyne, will need to go into the room, take her hand and walk into the past." (It truly got confusing with two Janynes, but this time she meant me.)

Yes, walking down the hallway meant I would become her (Jeannie?). The four of us could not go with her; we had to become her. We all had to become the child. When we did, there would not be anyone to protect her. The thought of what we would find there was terrifying. This was the fear Dr. Sue had seen on my face when I hit the panic button and locked the screaming child in the panic room.

Jane spoke up, "No, we couldn't go there tonight. We need Dr. Sue to go with her. She will protect her. She will hold us so we won't get more damaged."

Janyne chimed in, "It is all a bit curious. What do you think we will find there?"

I had wondered about this for months without accepting the probable truth. Janyne's curiosity was part of the reason we were all here. Her spirit had made us willing to take these leaps past reality. Non Janyne (who was really strong and smart) had gotten us to this point by thinking and planning. Jane now was figuring out how to care for little Jeannie as she hugged her puppy and slept. None of us had been willing to go where we were headed tomorrow … until now.

While talking with Dr. Sue the day before, an important question had arisen. "Dr. Sue, I don't think we will find a 'smoking gun' tomorrow. It doesn't make sense that there is some awful repressed memory. There could be, you know, but I don't think there is. But how did my mind fracture without some traumatic event?"

"Janyne, you did not have the foundational love of a mother to help you trust. You didn't have any choice but to trust her, but you learned you could not. Every parent makes mistakes, but they can be forgiven because of the bond of love. You did not have a bond, so it was hard to move past those things."

What she was saying made complete sense. Jeannie had done an astounding job of caring for herself, but she was living out of a vacuum. As I thought about this, it became clear that Jeannie had built schemas to live by, which appeared to be like what she observed in other "normal" families. She was going to take us back and show us, and we were going to try to help her understand. Understand what? I simply wasn't sure.

One thing was certain: we all needed sleep so we could face the day. The to-do list needed to vanish. We didn't need to go down the hallway and return home to undone things. I hoped we could all get some rest as we stood guard over Jeannie.

It was a long, fitful night. Jeannie slept well, but I could not. I tossed. I turned (always hugging the puppy). I got too hot and had to change pajamas. I had to get up and go to the bathroom. It seemed endless. Every time I settled back into bed, the three turned to me and said, "Shhhh, Jeannie is sleeping."

Where Jeannie Took Us

Jeannie slept long and hard. The three kept watch over her while my more functional self checked off the to-do list. She was still asleep when I reached the office to start the EMDR session.

As the door of the panic room opened, the four of us looked down on her. She was so peaceful; it was hard to wake her.

"Jeannie, Jeannie, it is time to wake up. We are all here. I am ready to follow you."

She sat up slowly and rubbed the sleep from her eyes. She looked around at all of us, a bit bewildered at first, then with understanding.

"Jeannie, are you ready for me to follow you?"

She was. She reached out and took my hand and we started down the hallway.

I slowly became the small child who was holding my hand. During the next hour, I walked in and out of memories. The Jeannie who led me there was four or five, but sometimes older, sometimes younger.

Jeannie stood looking at her mother after a car accident. She saw the large bruise on her mother's leg. She felt nothing. It seemed wrong to feel nothing, so she watched how others felt and learned to act as if she felt that way too.

Then Jeannie went to camp and had to ask why others were crying. "They miss their mothers." Missing Mother seemed logical, so Jeannie cried just so she could seem to miss her mother as the other girls did.

She didn't. Actually she was glad to be free from the constant expectations. She was trying so hard to be the perfect daughter, but she was little and no matter what she did, it was never enough.

JEANNIE BEGINS TO SPEAK

"I'm little, and I crawled into her lap and put my head on her shoulder. I had seen other children do this with their mothers, so I tried it. I felt nothing. It was uncomfortable. I never tried it again.

"I'm sick. My grandmother is staying with me. She has me sleep in her room so she can keep an eye on me. She brings me medicine. I feel so loved when someone wants to be close to me when I am sick. I never knew how it felt before."

"It feels good to be loved!" Dr. Sue's voice comforted me.

"Yes, it does. I'm at camp. I love camp. I get to spend a whole week with a counselor who is just there to pay attention to me. Sometimes I am bad just so I can wake up in the morning and see they still love me. They do.

"I am at church. There is an older man who greets me every Sunday. 'How are you today, Jeannie?'

"'I am fine!'

"'Do you want your candy today?'

"'Yes, I do!' I retrieve my piece of candy from his pocket and then I am off and running to find my friends."

"You felt loved by him."

"Yes, I did. Lots of people at church loved me.

"I ask and ask and get a bike; but no one will help me learn to ride it. I try again and again—for days, until I can ride it down the sidewalk. I am all battered and bruised, but I can ride and now I can be free. I can ride anywhere! I didn't need anyone to help me."

"You taught yourself!"

"Yes, but now I hurt and I have to stay home from school."

"Where is the pain? Can you feel the pain now?"

"Yes, I feel the pain. I feel it every day. It is a knot in my stomach. It is how I wake up every day. I am trying so hard to be perfect. I can't be perfect at home and at school. I can't do both."

Memory after memory, the picture was always the same. Jeannie was taking care of herself. She had no idea what it meant for a mother to love her, but she was doing her very best to be the daughter a mother would love. She felt absolutely nothing for the person everyone said was her mother. Nothing. Jeannie thought that was her fault. It wasn't.

"Can we go back to talk to the little girl? What would you like to tell her? Can you close your eyes and go back?"

Jeannie was back in the panic room, beckoning me.

Not wanting to follow her, I opened my eyes. My eyes begged Dr. Sue not to send me there, but her eyes were insistent. My eyes closed.

"I am standing by Jeannie in front of a gate." I had been to this gate often in my memory but had never gone in. Now Jeannie opened the gate, and we entered.

"I am little. I know I am little because the doll I am carrying is so big. She is hard for me to carry."

"How old are you?"

"I think I am three because the doll is so big. I am in a yard now. There are lots of toys in the yard—kind of strewn around like children have been playing there. I want to play but I need to go into the house. I walk in the door. It is dark and cold.

"The darkness grows. It gets bigger, heavier. I want to grab Jeannie and run, but she needs me to stay. I know she is trying to show me something, and we have to stay there to find out what it is. Something bad is happening to Jeannie. I am there with her under the huge dark heaviness. I can barely breathe. I am grabbing Jeannie, dragging her out of the house."

There was nothing to do but sink back into the couch and stare at the reality of the complete terror from which we had just escaped.

"I didn't expect to find anything. It wasn't my parents' fault. Sometimes you just need a place to keep the children. You think it's safe for them. You can't know this would happen. I don't know where this was, but I wasn't always there. I think I became very unhappy about being there and stayed outside and played. I kept myself safe."

"Yes, sometimes very bad things happen to children. You did learn how to take care of yourself."

"But I was so convinced it had not happened to me. I didn't want to be that person who went to therapy and found out something like this. I wanted my healing to just be about my mother. If my mother had been able to love me, I might have been able to recover in more healthy ways. I might have been able to tell her. I'm sure I didn't tell her. After this I did strange things for a small child to do. It makes sense now. I didn't want it to make sense. I don't want everything to be seen through this filter for the rest of his or her life. No one ever really believes these stories, because it happened when they were so small. How could they possibly even remember? They think the therapist led them to it—which is only logical."

My fears were unfounded. Even when she suspected sexual abuse, Dr. Sue never tried to lead me there.

"I tried not to go back to that place, but they sent me there anyway," I told Dr. Sue. "When I was in early elementary school, a little girl was killed. No one talked about it except in hushed whispers. But I knew what had happened to her. It made me feel very wise knowing something the adults would not tell me and would not expect me to know. I understood it could have been me, but it wasn't; and my freedom didn't need to be curtailed over something that didn't kill me. I knew how to take care of myself."

I needed to go back and talk to the small child inside the gate....

She's there, but she's playing. I call out to her across the yard. "Jeannie, I'm sorry I didn't listen. I'm sorry I didn't pay attention to what you were telling me. I did keep the puppy for you. We moved so much—twenty or more times, but I always kept the puppy. I was trying to take care of you, but I didn't know how to help you."

She wasn't listening, but she had stopped screaming.

How could I possibly walk away from this in any form that might be mistaken as functional? Dr. Sue sat and hugged me until the dissociative fog lifted and we felt it was safe for me to drive. Once home, I typed out my pain through a blur of tears. Finally, my body fell into a deep sleep, holding the puppy I had saved for so many years.

6
Working Through Layers

Having uncovered the abuse, our focus turned to working through layers that were affecting my daily life. First came acceptance of the fact that I had been abused as a small child. Then, came the work to integrate the three adult selves to the point that shifting from one to another was no longer a needed strategy. The ultimate goal was integration, but there was much to do before it could become a reality.

AFTER THE DEATH OF MY PERFECT LIFE

Following Jeannie down the hallway and through the gate was the final nail in the coffin of my "perfect life." There was no denying the carefully hidden dysfunction or the reason for the dysfunction. I was that person and it made me angry on multiple levels, none of which made much sense.

Maybe if the perpetrator had a face or an identity, my anger could have been focused there. This would probably never happen; it seemed Jeannie would have shown me if she could. She had worked so hard to bring me there and show me her fear and pain. Surely, she would have given me all the information if there had been more to give. My mind was not stopping her. (Well, it was, but I didn't know it at this point.)

Jeannie had found ways to walk through the fear and pain. My willingness to go there with her appeared to have finally set her free. There was nothing but understanding associated with this unexpected and tragic memory. For a while, it seemed possible to walk away unscathed.

Much to my surprise, I was not fine. I was less than fine. I was in a lake, paddling away from whirlpools and bailing water to keep from sinking. The tension, pain, and gnawing in the core of my being was almost unbearable. Why?

My thoughts on this were: *My strength makes me angry! It has kept me on my feet without any appearance of weakness my whole life. My stomach hurts from the pressure of being so strong. This unbelievable strength makes me angry. There is no room for me to be weak, but trying to pull it back together seems almost impossible. I want to switch places with Jeannie now. I want to be in the panic room. Please, let me curl up with the puppy and cry while someone pulls a blanket over me and sits down to watch over my sleeping body.*

But this really wasn't an option, was it? I had to live my life.

No Time To Heal

The apparent reconciliation of the Three Chairs, and their resolve to help my small-child self heal, seemed positive, but it was only a brief respite. I continued to reel from one therapy session to the next (lots of them), spent copious amounts of time curled up in fetal position and staring at walls. Some days it was impossible to get myself to walk out the front door. On one occasion, I got stuck in a parking lot and called Dr. Sue for help.

"Janyne, do you need to take some time off from work?"

The obvious answer was yes. The logical answer was yes. The answer my soul wanted was yes. The reality in my life was no. I could work from home. I could show up when necessary, rely on my good reputation or make excuses. But there was no time to heal—healing had to fit in around the edges.

Would it have been possible to take a "mental health break"? Making such a request and maintaining my credibility seemed unimaginable. My gender probably increased this reality. It was simply necessary to process at lightning speed and believe I could come out on the other end still standing.

Almost every day, I managed to get up and walk through the day. Early mornings, during the night, and weekends found me digging through boxes of memories, reading journals, and processing. I wrote page after page after page in the yellow note-pads.

In the midst, there were family events, holidays, meetings, and work. There just was not a "put life on hold" button anywhere. I looked for it. I longed for it, but it was not any-where to be found. Some days found me falling off cliffs. Other days, whirlpools were swallowing me. I cried in my sleep and dreamed horrible dreams. But in the midst of surviving life, there came clues, peaceful breakthroughs, clarifying realiza-tions, and support from Scott and Dr. Sue.

Moving this quickly through therapy would never be my recommendation. It was crazy and terrifying. I am thankful for a therapist who never flinched and believed in my instincts, but she always had concern about pushing too hard. At this point in my life, there seemed to be no other way.

A sense of safety to access help should have been possible much earlier in my life. What happened to me wasn't border-line—you know, "maybe therapy would be good or maybe not." No, my story screamed the need for help, but there had never been freedom to access therapy. Nothing in my life or current situation led me to believe openly telling the truth would result in anything but more pain.

Little and All Grown Up at the Same Time

As layers of pain continued to erupt, I forced myself to be functional for four-hour stretches, only to collapse in a heap of exhaustion and emotion. It was during this fragile time when mold was discovered in our condo. Without strength or resistance, I developed debilitating bronchial asthma. In some ways this was actually helpful. I had a reason to be sick and stay home. Naps could be taken on my office couch at the end of my four-hour functional period. Blessed peaceful sleep could be gained with codeine cough syrup.

All of this, on top of trying to help a small-child self, brought me to therapy in an exhausted daze. The physical distress was awful, but the mental anguish was worse.

"You are a little girl right now and she is having a hard time functioning in your adult world."

Thank you, Dr. Sue. The idea of trying to function as a small child never occurred to me.

"How can I help her?"

"Tell her you are going to work, but you will be back. Leave her there in a place where she feels safe. Let her know you are going to take care of her."

This is how Jeannie and I came to an agreement about life. Sometimes it was necessary to go be an adult. While an adult, she needed to feel safe. After all these years, she needed me to be her mother—a mother who would listen to her, love her, protect her, and give her reassurance when she needed it.

The guest bedroom was a perfect place to put her picture and each morning I talked to her and told her the plan for the day. In addition, her picture was on my cell phone so she could sometimes come with me and experience my grown up world. Finally, when we crawled into bed, the puppy was in our arms. There really was nothing I was unwilling to do to help this remarkable little child who had been very brave to take me down the hallway, through the gate, and into the dark ominous cloud so the pain could be understood and we could heal together.

Every night I said, "Good night, little Jeannie. Sleep the deep peaceful sleep of a child who feels loved and protected. I am hugging the puppy and listening to you."

My Journey of Shame

Most palpable in my daily living was the feeling of dread over the most innocuous and simple things. There was either dread for the future, dread afterwards based on my performance, or panic in the midst of the event. When Non Janyne was tightly in control, she was able to make me walk through this horribly inconvenient side of my psyche. Now she was no longer the controlling factor in my life, and this part of me was just running rampant.

Between caring for a small child, working on the team spirit of the Three Chairs, and dealing with an ever-increasing level of anxiety and dread, I was exhausted. Playing games on my cell phone or working jigsaw puzzles provided a way to escape. It also appeared to free some part of my brain to process. I became trapped in an almost impossible "jigsaw puzzle." I was obsessed. My obsession was apparent to everyone, but I just didn't know what to do about it.

The missing piece to the puzzle and the key to the growing dread were found simultaneously—it was shame. Cognitively, this made perfect sense. Insecure attachment, abuse, betrayal, and an abundance of incorrect self perceptions had created shame. Shame was the belief that there was something dreadfully wrong with me.

Why hadn't I acknowledged this as the culprit? (The shame was evident to Dr. Sue from the beginning of therapy, but it was at the core of the feelings I rejected. It took time for me to accept these feelings.)

We needed to help the child who had obviously experienced shame. A picture of me at about six, sitting under the table, provided a starting point. My memories had often placed me under the table. Why was I hiding?

"I am under the table. I feel safe here. I am hiding. My mother is walking by. She walks very fast. She is always busy. Clip clop, clip clop. She passes by me again and again. I am hiding because I am invisible."

I realized I was whispering.

"You fear she will see you there." Dr. Sue was also whispering.

"I don't want her to see me here. I have probably done something wrong. I don't want her to notice me. She will be angry with me."

"You did something."
Silence....

"I try hard to be good. I'm a good girl. I don't want to cause problems. I just can't do things right. I don't know what isn't right, but I know she disapproves. I don't know why."

We followed trails, we worked through levels of anxiety from childhood to adult, but the conclusion was the same. There didn't seem to be any particular reason why the anxiety was drowning me (though Dr. Sue later told me she suspected it was connected to additional memories of the abuse at the day care).

There it was. As a child there was no way to tell what I was doing wrong, what brought the disapproval. It must be everything. I was told I embarrassed her. The assumption was it was me who could do nothing right. I was trying, on guard and ashamed of myself—all of me—who I was on any given day.

Despite hypervigilance, I had no way to discern what the problem was. Even my best efforts received criticism, but I never knew why, and there was no one to blame for the failure but myself. Therefore, everything was dreaded, because there was always potential for failure. No matter how good the job was, there was always something wrong with it. There was always a reason to beat myself up upon completion. This was my everyday experience.

This realization astounded me. The movie of my life began scrolling. Every instance when I spoke, or made a phone call, or drove across town and made a wrong turn, was potentially shameful. Every single day of my life ended with a replay of my failures.

This understanding of hypervigilance made me wonder if my older brother's experience had been the same.

"How did you feel at home with mother?" I asked him.

"I felt I had to be on guard about everything. There was no pleasing her."

Since I had been unable to come up with anything specific myself, I asked, "Like what? What did you feel you did wrong?"

His answer mirrored my own experience, "I don't know. I can't remember anything, any memory. It was just knowing there wasn't anything I could do right."

Me too. The ever-present inability to please is why this sense of dread and shame was so pervasive. There was no memory. No specific incident caused it. It was ever present then, and it was ever present now.

DREAD, SHAME, AND ANGER

Understanding there was nothing specific to account for the feeling of dread was huge. This pervasive feeling, which infected every area of my life, really did start somewhere—and everywhere. This made it so difficult to heal. There was no way go to a specific memory in EMDR and remove its power over me. We did work through the shame attached, but the triggers were everywhere, and it became necessary to talk myself down from every one of them.

There was great celebration for successful moments when a trigger was overcome without cognitively thinking myself away from hypervigilance. The examples were as commonplace as leaving a phone message or sending an email. They were everywhere in my life.

As time went by, the unbelievable strain under which I had lived became clear. My ability to have lived a professional life under this paradigm was nothing less than miraculous; but living life abundantly wasn't possible with this level of anxiety and dread.

Anger was another issue. One day, the evidence of trying to live a functional life without Non Janyne's control burst forth with the clear attitude of my very unhappy seventh-grade self. There was no way to stop the emotional train wreck. What appeared to be terror gripped me as I desperately tried to end a phone conversation with Dr. Sue. There was anger because, like the seventh grader, my needs were not being met due to something beyond my control; but this did not explain the terror.

I knew this anger. It was never clear where it came from or how violently it escalated. I feared it because it had ruined a relationship in high school. It had been tightly controlled ever since.

The difficult phone conversation with my therapist convinced me that anger needed to be addressed. I had always considered the scripture verse about being angry but not sinning as a guide. Anger wasn't the problem if controlled appropriately. The degree to which my anger escalated was not sin; it was something deeper. To blame this level of anger on sin was a church "go to," but less than effective in truly helping and freeing a person.

When trapped in situations that escalated my anger, I refused to stay even when I was requested to stay. Anger mixed with fear was a debilitating experience. When these feelings escaped, others probably perceived it as only anger, but it wasn't—it was terror. In those moments, the trapped little girl inside of me was fighting for her life.

Back in therapy, EMDR cut apart anger and fear with the precision of a sharply-honed knife. For the first time, fear was recognizable and anger was a pure emotion. I wrote:

> *Anger, felt alone without fear, is a pure, clear emotion. It is the expression of the injustice of the situation. The expression doesn't continue to escalate; it is articulate and defining; it proclaims the truth of the feeling. It doesn't attack in damaging ways—it makes the statement and is done.*

It was so freeing to finally understand the verse about being angry and not sinning. It was possible to just be angry, to express anger without fear or rage, to have a voice. It was going to take practice, but I was free from the automatic escalation.

However, this did not mean the fear was gone.

LIVING WITH FEAR

My journey with anger made me realize my fear was literally

because I was afraid of being my mother. She had suffered from intense paranoia that had affected our lives in untold ways. My fear was of the possibility of my continuing this pattern. Non Janyne had always made me walk through my fear of almost everything. Agoraphobia could have been a possibility without this part of me. As Non Janyne's control lessened, the instances when it seemed impossible to walk out the door increased.

Was I afraid of what was outside the door? No, it wasn't exactly fear of what was outside. It appeared to be a fear of being my mother while I was out walking around in the world. My life had been devoted to not being my mother, and now it wasn't clear whether or not I had the strength to keep up this struggle.

My need to be "stellar" grew out of thinking my mother's same level of dysfunction existed in me. I was not going to let it affect my life or do damage to others. My not being dysfunctional was a way of proving she did not have to damage others. It was not a need to be perfect; it was survival. My definition of survival was being someone who lived my life without allowing the dysfunction (whatever it was) to show.

Eventually, as my mind let carefully-hidden memories come out, it was clear the dysfunction had roots. I had been a bright, happy child. I wasn't born defective. My mother probably had not been, either, and there was value in understanding this, but that was hard for me to accept. Most importantly, there was value in understanding my daily fear, and how the fear was related to my life with my own mother. I never felt safe in her presence.

If I were like her, then I couldn't feel safe in my own presence. This was a whole new layer of hypervigilance. I was afraid my own ill-chosen words, awkward moments, or ill-timed actions were more signs of my inherited dysfunction. As

I processed my childhood through therapy, awareness grew that I did not feel safe with myself. It was essential to prove I was not my mother.

Non Janyne Is My Mother

Then came the epiphany that Non Janyne was created in the image of my mother—a stunning realization. This had never occurred to me. When Janyne and Jane got into trouble, Non Janyne was created to control them and everything my mother had believed about me was confirmed—left to my own devices, I was just going to get into trouble. Why my mother believed this was hidden until my college freshman memory surfaced—a year and a half later.

While considering this revelation, all the ways in which Non Janyne acted like my mother were astounding. She rejected the infant and the needy Jane. She was mostly disapproving of Janyne's boisterous nature. She followed rules and expected everyone else to do so. She was very concerned about appearances. She was strong, tenacious and determined. She tried to avoid stressful situations, but was always busy accomplishing more than seemed possible for any human.

It was true—I had become the person I was afraid of being. I could not grasp this! As my mind began to disentangle the one I had made myself to be from my true self, it became obvious there was no inherited dysfunction.

I was not, am not, and will not ever be my mother. It was not necessary to be more this or more that. Just being me was fine. People loved me. They did not love who I was not. With this epiphany, the debilitating fear of simply being me ended.

"Dr. Sue, can I be rewired?"

The answer was always yes.

7
Healing an Infant

We were now months into what I had thought would be done in a few sessions. The idea of getting to the place of being "done" gave me hope. But as soon as one layer was peeled back, another would appear, and I would find myself desperate for help once again. It was embarrassing.

Dr. Sue tried to help me be nice to myself. "Janyne, there are so many layers to work through. Some people work through a layer and then stop for a while and come back when another layer surfaces. What you have done would normally take years. I don't think you know any other speed."

She was right. I didn't know any other speed. My processing was relentless. Part of this was because of the desire for answers, but mostly it was because the pain had been released into my daily life. It was impossible to live my life with the level of pain I was experiencing. It was terrifying. The pain had been right under the surface my entire life; now it was loose. It had to be contained—or healed. The years of containing the pain had exhausted me. Healing was my desperate hope, and necessitated moving toward the goal.

Occasionally, the process of peeling back layers brought glimpses of wellness. These tended to create false hopes that the end had been reached. I had actually only visited those things already known to be true so they could be seen in a different way. My interpretation of my childhood had been incorrect.

Reinterpreting my childhood was important; but my very early wiring continued to affect me every single day.

In order to integrate, we would need to heal an infant.

IT BEGINS IN THE CRIB

My expression for emotional collapse was always that I was falling off a cliff. It always landed me in bed. It would be another year before we understood the underlying truth of the cliff.

On one particular day, a Saturday afternoon, self loathing was running away with me and I had no structures in place to control my emotions. I was in trouble. It seemed my previous dependent relationships had been traded in for a new one— with my therapist. This was necessary in order to make progress, but progress was not particularly evident on this miserable day.

In bed and tortured, the level of anger I felt toward myself frightened me. Scott called for help. Try as I might to fight it, he was right to call. The dependency I was loathing also made me want to go to therapy.

I was a self-loathing, sixty-one-year-old infant who needed a mother. Everyone was trying to rescue me. It could not have been more humbling.

The memories, which aided in the healing of the infant, are detailed in Part III, but the healing began inside the journey of the Three Chairs. Insecure attachment as an infant results in life-long patterns. It also makes a child susceptible to abuse. Perpetrators know how to spot these children who so desperately needed to attach during infancy. Their psyches were wired to seek attention, and their inability to do so with their mothers can reap tragic results.

FACE TO FACE, STILL FACE

Early in my years of studying child development, I came

across research describing the interactions between infants and caregivers. In the experiment by Dr. Edward Tronick (1975), babies were placed face to face with their mothers who, after initially talking to the children, then expressed no emotion and made no eye contact. Videos of the experiment demonstrated how children, who did not receive appropriate reactions, first attempted various strategies to connect, but when met with failure eventually showed signs of extreme distress. The videos (available online) caused me to feel very uncomfortable.

In one EMDR experience, which took me to the crib, I was unable to illicit eye contact with my mother. The still-face experiment seemed to explain my futile attempts at engagement. I began to watch videos with the sinking realization that the still face was my infant reality. When initial attempts to engage my mother did not elicit a reaction, my clever infant self initiated multiple engagement strategies—smiling, reaching out, and babbling. When these failed, the distress was evident. My infant self did everything she could to engage, but her brain became wired to accept failure.

In normal situations, "still face" does happen to some degree. A mother cannot always be attentive to her child. This becomes part of teaching the child to self soothe. This works well when the mother keeps returning to engage the child; but when that doesn't happen, the child is not able to fully or effectively develop self regulation and soothing strategies. The result is lifelong attachment issues and dysfunctional relationship patterns. Attachment disorder has not been identified as an adult disorder (unfortunately), but the symptoms from insecure attachment exhibit in a myriad of other diagnoses. In those cases, treating adult symptoms outside of the attachment context does not address the root cause.

Yes, I came to understand this. But cognitive knowledge

and rewiring are not the same thing. The attachment cycle was my life pattern and always led me to the edge of an emotional cliff. The inherent shame involved in being unable to control this early wiring only added to the distress. This precarious state was exactly what was happening, and everyone was trying to help me.

In therapy we had returned to the crib more than once and still I knew we had not fully solved the problem. During these memories there were a few peaceful moments amidst my attempts to engage my mother. My oldest brother's face would appear over the top of the crib, and there was a look of interest in his eyes. He was and still is watching over me, as part of my village. He and my dad prevented even greater damage to the small soul whose mother was unable to look at her and smile.

This early wiring caused the most intensive phase of my therapy, which made sense because it was embedded in my earliest attempts at forming an identity. It was intense and I desperately tried to come out on the other side. Dr. Sue and Scott did all they could to help me keep walking. In several extended therapy sessions good progress was made. I thought the self loathing had dissipated, when suddenly something rose up inside of me—something that defied explanation. We would not realize it was the exhausted Gatekeeper (part of my dissociative system) until much later.

REPELLED BY AN INFANT

Even after so much progress, from my adult perspective this infant was the root problem. All these months in therapy were the fault of this dysfunctional part of me, which simply could not engage appropriately in life. At the moment when my adult self got a clear look at the infant, I suddenly attacked her. This was so surprising! Hadn't Jane been caring for her?

Hadn't the Three Chairs protected her? Why did I attack her?

She is standing there naked in front of me! I am her judge. I am angry with her for holding me captive all these years. She was the cause of everything. We don't need her. She will drag us down, slow us down. We don't need her little hypervigilant self watching our every move. We are done with panic attacks, going to bed, and searching endlessly for someone to see us/love us when our life is filled with those people. We are done with her needy little self.

This scene exploded out of me in a stunning way. So this was how my adult self was viewing the damaged central core of my soul? How tragic. Where did this come from? In an effort to regain the controls, I began writing again: "Stop! She is an infant/three year old. She doesn't deserve to be viewed as just a needy adult!"

If viewed as a small child, she made perfect sense. What seemed awkward for an adult was normal for a child. I realized these parts of me were perfectly normal for a child:

- She had separation anxiety.
- She needed attention, touch, gazing.
- She was constantly trying to engage others to pay attention to her.
- She manipulated circumstances to get her needs met.
- She would shut down from excessive stimulation.
- She was unable to care for herself; she needed others to care for her.
- Small tasks appeared monumentally difficult.
- She was uncomfortable in new situations.
- She was afraid of being alone.
- She threw temper tantrums over interrupted plans.

Some of those elements were horribly awkward in my adult world but made perfect sense for a small child trying to exist as an adult. My thinking began to change like a computer game of solitaire when it becomes clear you are winning and the game takes over. I could actually feel my brain change while I wrote, "I am a perfectly normal child who needs to find adult coping strategies. These problems are not because of some defect."

With this paradigm shift, my hatred for the small child dissipated. She needed help to find healthy ways to function. She needed me to care for her and help her learn to live in ways not based on survival. She needed to learn to care for herself without using manipulation. This small child needed me to truly see and help her.

Healing a Small Human

As the pieces slowly surfaced and healed, Dr. Sue and I felt we were close to integration of the Three Chairs. The shifting had become less pronounced and the three were working as a team. We had tried to accomplish final integration through this new acceptance of each other, but had been met with the angry outburst concerning the infant. The tension was difficult to understand until I recognized the separation between my outer and inner life. We were trying to cross the borders between the "me" who had always existed on the outside and the "me" who I truly was inside. At the core was a small hurting human who had always been rejected.

Like opposite pole magnets, the two sides were repelling each other. They were never coming together because the newly integrating Janyne continued to be repelled by the pain still evident inside the infant. The hurting child felt this rejection—it was no different from the rejection she had always felt.

The therapy sessions had been intense; but even after this paradigm shift, still no resolution appeared. Suddenly, the small human seemed to intuitively understand this rejection and what it would take to heal her pain. She stepped out courageously and begged to be held, to be wrapped in the only thing that would help her: complete acceptance. She asked to be held and Dr. Sue held her.

While being wrapped in complete acceptance, I sensed my mind unwinding rejection and receiving acceptance. Every small human needs this feeling of complete acceptance. It was as if my mind was reviewing the child development texts I had taught for years. Children needed:

- Complete security.
- Gentle care/touch.
- Playful interaction.
- Unconditional love.
- Desire to connect.
- Eagerness to know and understand them.
- Joy in discovering their amazing gifts and attributes.
- Delight in the unfolding of their personality.
- Belief and expectation for their future.
- Willingness to totally invest in helping a small human become all they can be.
- Self sacrifice joyfully given, not out of obligation but sincere desire.

This description was what my small human self had needed from my mother but never received. It is what would have wired her correctly, but it did not happen. The place in my soul where a mother's acceptance belonged was a complete waste-land. As my sobbing adult self was held, the realization of full acceptance poured over my inner pain. My soul would never be the same because it had finally been seen and not rejected.

"Dr. Sue, the Three Chairs are ready. I don't think they will be repelled by my infant core anymore." My eyes closed as I returned to the crib.

Lifting the small human from the crib, I held her tightly and began rocking. The parts of my soul began to merge. The fractured pieces began to come together as if in a gigantic puzzle. I felt each one snap in place, forever locking the small child in the arms of my integrated self. Then, as I felt God reach down and hold me in his hands, I sensed the final connection like a vacuum seal locks a door in place. I felt wholeness.

8
Three Chairs Integration

In comparison to months of chaos, living life was becoming easier. It felt good. I had become comfortable with the Three Chairs in their new integrated form and thought it might be possible to just live my life that way. Though working hard to feel like one whole person, there was occasionally a sense of shifting, which I didn't fully understand. Despite this, the completely nonfunctional episodes were almost nonexistent, and it seemed possible that full integration had been reached in less than a year.

TRYING TO LIVE LIFE AGAIN

My life was busy and I had much to look forward to, including several trips. Lingering anxiety caused some concern, but I felt this could be worked through before the traveling began. Perhaps that was the Janyne part of me who was full of optimism and hope, but it felt good. My new confident self began to consider ending therapy. Maybe a break to process what had been accomplished would be beneficial.

Since the day we discovered the three, integration was the goal. Though the new alliance between the Three Chairs felt comfortable, it couldn't be labeled as mentally "healthy" in any sense of the word. The ever-present sense of dread was still there every morning. Something—actually, a lot—was missing.

What integration meant to me at this point was still

probably more like survival than wholeness. My greatest desire was for the constant buzz of conversations in my head to stop so I could be functional for more than four-hour stretches. There was a need to feel a degree of control over some portion of my life. The inherent wisdom of leaping down the rabbit hole in my head was still under discussion. Everything I feared my entire life had finally come true; but I somehow managed to live through the pain; so there was hope for better days ahead.

All the while, on the very back burner of the therapy stove was the decision about signing my contract for the following year. This next section, written sometime later, opens a window into my feelings during this complex period of trying to heal, continuing to work, living my life, and needing to make a decision.

Over Easy with a Touch of Paranoia

My food sat before me waiting for consumption. It was breakfast in bed—a seldom-experienced luxury over the years, but one I was enjoying on this day. In the center of the plate was my toast and next to it a perfectly cooked egg—over easy. As I gently lifted the egg onto the toast, my mouth watered, and my stomach growled.

As the yolk began to ooze from its fragile membrane, my mind reflected. *That is exactly the feeling! I am oozing. Can anyone tell? Yep, this is how I feel, over easy with a touch of paranoia.*

It was disconcerting to realize my carefully constructed shell was no longer very effective. I had worked so hard to keep it intact. The smile, the laugh, the "stellarness," the carefully chosen words—all of it effectively hid the pain inside me for over fifty years. But now I was definitely oozing and most assuredly paranoid about it.

It happened in a faculty meeting. I had attended faculty

meetings for thirty years and was pretty much over them. Sometimes important things happened; but most often I wished they had sent me an email. Of course, the email probably would not have been read very carefully, and the dean knew this; so it was undoubtedly necessary to make me sit in the meeting—which was tolerable until someone hijacked the discussion with an obvious agenda.

Everything in me screamed, *Really? You are going there? Again?*

Since these seemed very inappropriate words to blurt out, I learned to sink deeper in my chair and wait it out.

One day I didn't sink. I'm not sure why. Some unsinkable thing inside me—some part of me wanted to yell, *Stop it!* Instead, another part of me tried to engage on an intellectual level. But I appeared to be the only one on that level. Finally, with a huge sigh of frustration, the unsinkable part of me said, "You know, I am just not playing well with others today."

What?

Did they see it?

Instant paranoia.

I was oozing.

The oozing had been happening for several years, but the cracking of the fragile membrane around the yolk had been a recent development. I had committed the great sin of going to therapy and had landed in some kind of double agent, secret life. I was hiding in plain sight while my inner life imploded. Why not just be open about it and ask for prayer? Maybe they would send out a memo to the campus asking for prayer for my mental breakdown. Maybe they would start a fund to help me pay for the sessions I wasn't claiming on insurance. Maybe there was a bridge in Brooklyn someone might buy from me.

No. None of those options were possible realities.

As a consummate professional and a master teacher, I had many diplomas and awards in my office. There were also plaques for multiple years of service and a curriculum vita worthy of honor. I was a lot of really awesome things including a wife who had been married thirty-six years and a mother with two accomplished children, a remarkable daughter-in-law, and two precious grandchildren. What I was not was a therapy client who had experienced early childhood sexual abuse and survived her life with a dissociative disorder. Being in intensive therapy and trying to save the life I had built, but now wasn't sure I wanted, seemed all but impossible. Yes, I was oozing.

And I was absolutely paranoid.

Looking at the breakfast egg oozing on my toast, I knew I had no choice but to resign. God knew it. My husband knew it. My family knew it. My closest friends knew it. My therapist knew it. Worst of all, I knew it. I didn't accept it, but I knew it.

How would we survive? How would we pay for the therapy? How would I explain the unexplainable to those who had no right or reason to know the truth? How would I get up and look at myself every day? What would make me crawl out of the bed?

There it was. The bed. There was something about my bed and the sense of overwhelming dread, which greeted me every morning. I would lie there and ooze until I pulled my layers around me and found someone to live the day.

"Let's see, today we need to be all professional and get lots of work done—this persona will do nicely."

It took me months to realize this was happening and now even without shifting, the dread remained. If I resigned, who would get up in the morning? Me? I was moving toward feeling more integrated but didn't necessarily want to spend copious days doing nothing with the one who was emerging.

Continuing to reflect on the oozing egg in front of me, it seemed, as difficult as being with me every day might be, resigning was far better than oozing in a public forum. It was clear the new me emerging was not someone able to sit in faculty meetings. I simply could not play well with others anymore. I was done—over easy, but done—and definitely paranoid. There was no other choice but to resign.

SLOWLY REBUILDING

During this phase I wrote volumes of pages. The important threads are included here in abridged form. Some of the specific childhood memories are told in the Part IV stories of the children. Up to this point in therapy, we had no idea children were actually beginning to surface and tell us carefully chosen memories in order to help the three adults heal and integrate.

The process of integration was long and complex and beyond telling within this story. What is included provides adequate background to understand the pain, fear, and endless processing. Despite all the hard work, there was minimal awareness of the extent of the abuse that had occurred at age three. It amazes me that my psyche understood that the adult "me" needed to integrate before the children could safely surface.

As this phase of therapy wound down, the primary goal was to find and heal the pieces, which were preventing a sense of wholeness. Some of those pieces involved childhood and teen memories, but most centered on the healing of the infant described earlier. When the three adults finally embraced my small-child self, their separateness began to dissipate.

The process of creating a replacement for the Three Chairs had begun, but this fact was completely outside my awareness. All I knew was after the day we healed the infant, being completely fractured in three parts vanished from my sense of self.

Still, living with so much "differentness" inside me presented a challenge.

In hindsight, the amount of healing that had to take place before I could even begin to understand there were over fifteen children, teen, and young adult alters waiting in the wings, is truly astounding. It is also hard to comprehend how this deeply painful layer was only an outer shell, hiding the memories of over ten episodes of sexual abuse. It was essential to integrate and stabilize as one adult before I could survive what was coming next.

By spring I was stronger and life was calling. I needed to be functional for a while. It was time for graduation, and everyone believed I was retiring. There was a chance of a new job, but no assurance. Retirement seemed like a distinct but unsettling possibility. With only slight uneasiness about doing so, I took a break from therapy.

My Day of Triumph!

The day for graduation and retirement had arrived. While standing in the line of faculty and waiting for the music to begin, I knew this would be the last processional in my graduation regalia. After thirty-three years, I had promised myself this day would end the era. Graduations weren't a problem—I always enjoyed them. To see students who had battled discouragement, exhaustion, hardship, self doubt, and sometimes depression walk across the stage and receive diplomas was my favorite part of being on faculty. No, graduation was wonderful.

But I hated triggers.

On this day, I didn't fully know my story, but enough had surfaced for me to understand I had lived as multiples with debilitating depression and what would prove to be PTSD symptoms. Despite this, almost everything on my life list had been accomplished. It was time to retire.

Yes, I had finished well. This had been the goal all year long. Only one or two attending the graduation knew my year had been spent in intensive therapy. Almost all were unaware that on some days my husband had to come back home to help me get up the stairs and out the door. They also did not know of the days when he had to call my therapist for intervention. No one knew because when I walked onto the campus, none of this was visible. They wondered why I was retiring.

The line began to move. My body braced itself. *Here we go.* I had identified the spot on the program where I would be honored. It ruined the day, because it required me to wait for my turn—an emotional trigger that had always been with me, though I didn't yet understand its cause.

The processional ended and my body sank into the chair in relief. Someone was talking to me when suddenly a colleague behind me gave me a nudge. "They're calling you."

This prompted a complete panic attack, which sent me forward with the all too familiar tunnel vision. I smiled. I listened to the accolades. I received my very large Dr. Seuss card (kind of odd but it made sense) and acknowledged the first standing ovation of my life.

Inside my soul, I was giving myself my own personal standing ovation. I had done it. I had finished well. I had lived out my life without anyone ever knowing the darkness, which threatened to consume me every day. There was nothing left undone—every task had been completed with excellence. My devotion to my family and students was always clear.

Yes, I had finished well. But the familiar gray fog, through which I viewed my life, was still there. My husband stood ready to take my picture. I wanted to cry, but crying was always a dangerous, open-the-floodgates thing to do. So I smiled instead—the most triumphant smile of a lifetime!

MOVING FORWARD

'I could tell you my adventures—beginning from this morning,' said Alice a little timidly: 'but it's no use going back to yesterday, because I was a different person then.'

–Alice

It appeared the "other side" had been reached. While not feeling completely whole, I was certainly no longer the person who said, "Which one?"

Like Alice, I was a different person in many significant ways.

My life needed to pause, and I needed to take a breath. Therapy wrapped up, I gave Dr. Sue a symbolic gift and said "Thank you," desperately wanting to believe it was finished. Time to organize my thoughts about what actually happened the day I fell down the rabbit hole. Stabilization was a must!

Delving into research about dissociation had been avoided to a great degree because of my tendency to make everything about my brain instead of my soul. The only way my fractured brain (and soul) would ever heal would be by my willingness to listen to the hurting voices inside me. Nevertheless, by this time I had a very clear understanding of dissociative disorders—the reasons for fracturing and the typical structures.

While organizing my thoughts, continuing to struggle to effectively handle emotional distress, and facing a daunting summer, I took several deep breaths and headed into my uncertain future. It appeared I was fine—until I wasn't.

ALL NEAT AND TIDY—AND SHATTERED

I imagined complete healing had been accomplished. I

had found the cause of my fracturing and healed my mother wounds. The three adult selves had integrated and were preparing to head out and begin my new life as a healthy, whole human. I felt whole. But something was not quite right.

This peaceful feeling was brought to me by my amazing ability to create alters. I took all the parts of me I liked, and built a new me. I wrote a description of her and found it much later in my files. Hundreds of miles were walked as I wired her into my brain. She truly believed the new job she had applied for was hers. She was building all the skills she needed to succeed in the job—and she would have done it. Healing had brought me to the point where it was possible—for a while.

Then, one fateful day, while sitting in my car outside a restaurant, I received the "we have gone another direction" email regarding the job for which I had applied. The email jumped out at me from my phone and shock reverberated through my body. I looked up and saw my perfect new "me" fall to the sidewalk and shatter into a thousand pieces. Like shards of glass glittering in the afternoon sun, my inner structures began to shred my soul.

I don't remember driving home.

9
Trying to Survive

I really had retired. I wasn't the amazing new creation I expected to be—the one who was headed to a new job. My daughter and grandchildren were moving. My dad was in a nursing home, trying to live to his 100th birthday. We couldn't continue living in the place we had rented to care for him. We had tried to move him to Arizona to be nearer more relatives, but this hadn't happened. Crying in front of the Social Security office was humiliating, and my exhausted body wondered what to do with the boxes filled with the remnants of a life I could no longer live. It was a fragile time. It only took one text message about possibly moving away from my dad to send me back to bed. I didn't eat for a week unless Scott made me. He was concerned.

My head was screaming for help, begging Scott to call Dr. Sue, but my words said the opposite. I was in trouble. Asking for help or accepting help seemed impossible. All my words and actions were exactly the opposite of what my shattered soul needed.

Dr. Sue's words haunted me. "You know, we are ending therapy today, but if you need help in the future you can always return. You understand, right?"

Oh, yes, it was an option, but one that wouldn't be needed. I had felt the insecurity inside of me but convinced myself it was just part of becoming independent. Everything was going to be just fine. But then when everything wasn't fine, returning to therapy felt impossible.

"Are you done with therapy?" These words in Dr. Sue's email jumped off the computer screen. My soul cried in agony. After days of avoiding the truth, I finally called for help, and began the tortured waiting for a return call. It came while I was driving.

"Can you talk, Janyne?"

"Yes. Let me navigate off this busy street first."

I had forced myself out of bed to go check on my dad, and had started to eat again, but was about as miserable as I'd ever been since falling down the rabbit hole.

"You asked me if I was done with therapy."

"Are you?"

"I want to say yes, but being in bed for a week and not eating probably wouldn't seem like it was true. I would be there still but life forced me out of bed. The bed calls me every waking moment of the day."

"Do you need to make an appointment?"

Oh, dear God, no! I feel like such a failure! I was done. I was so confident. I would have been OK if my life hadn't come apart.

The sobs lurked in my throat, but my desire for normal kept them there. Controlling my emotions, I carefully continued. "It is the stress in my life—the circumstances and huge decisions I have to make. I just can't seem to stay on top of it."

"Let's make an appointment. Can you come to see me Wednesday?"

My soul was screaming. This mess was not fair to Scott. I was putting him through hell—again. There was so much needing to be packed but my body was paralyzed most of the time. Suddenly, my heart convulsed because I no longer had a job to pay for therapy. Scott would say not to worry, but it was unrealistic.

"Just come to the appointment, Janyne. You are not done."

Swallowing Shards of Glass

It had come to this.

"Arrive at 4:45 and come straight into my office, then you won't have to sit in the waiting room."

Walking back into therapy was probably the hardest thing I had done since my first day of therapy so many months before. Like a frightened kitten, I sat on the therapist's couch and tried to avoid eye contact.

"You don't want to be here."

"No. Piece by piece, everything in my life has been stripped from me—except my family. At least it's not like Job—he even lost his family. And today, my pride is stripped from me."

It felt like I was swallowing those shards of glass that had exploded all over the sidewalk. This "me" was so far from the energetic, engaging Janyne who had sat on the couch with such confidence the first day of therapy.

"It's OK to come back. You weren't done. Can you see that?"

"Well, it's pretty obvious, isn't it?" My anger surprised me.

"Yes."

"I wanted to be done and be the amazing client who was rewired and off to live a new life. But there is no new life to live. I thought there would be. The sermon Sunday was about Abraham taking Isaac up the hill to sacrifice him. He told the servants, 'Wait until we return.' See? He didn't really think God was going to make him sacrifice his child. Every step he took up the mountain was hard, but he believed he wouldn't have to do it. This is like what happened to me. I resigned, but it never occurred to me there wasn't going to be a lamb in the thicket. There wasn't; and the knife plunged into my career. And now I am on the couch again."

The feeling of failure was overwhelming.

"What you have accomplished is amazing, but it doesn't mean you were done. It is OK to need more help. So, you think this is about the job falling through?"

"I don't really think so. I resigned in obedience to God and have complete peace about leaving; but am just lost now because there is no purpose, no goal, and no future."

Suspecting I would be asked about the last statement, I continued, "Well, yes, there is a future. I just can't see it."

"That's right. You can't see it right now."

Sitting quietly for a moment, the memory of the text message returned.

"It really started with the text."

"The text?"

I explained what happened. "But I don't understand why that sent me to bed. It just felt so uncaring, considering the decisions that must be made right now."

"Do you want to do therapy with those decisions and see if it will help you?"

That was a starting place, and my soul was screaming for relief. The memory my soul gave up, though, was not at all expected....

"I'm in bed. I can't move. I can't eat. I'm crying."

"How old are you?"

"I am every age. I've been there again and again. I am in my forties, in my twenties, now I am a teenager. No wait, I am in first grade. No I am still younger—I am three."

Something was happening to me. I went silent. My voice was silent, but my body was not. I wasn't fighting; the sensations were not unpleasant, but they made me uncomfortable. I began crying out as I felt the searing pain inside of me.

"It hurts! Why are you hurting me? You said you weren't hurting me, but it hurts. Stop hurting me!"

I began floating above the pain. It was the cloud, the darkness I had come to know so intimately. There was no pain in the darkness. It was hiding the pain below it, keeping me safe.

I stared into Dr. Sue's eyes. "We got there, didn't we?"

"Yes." She nodded and waited.

I continued processing. It seemed the memory had never been fully processed. I knew it was true. There had been acceptance that "something" happened when Jeannie took me through the gate—but I had never fully accepted it was *this*. I was oddly OK. It was true. I felt peaceful. An almost emotionless peacefulness.

FLOATING ABOVE THE PAIN

The small yellow notepads were back again. It was frustrating. No, I wasn't done. Yet, maybe since it felt so peaceful at the end of the session… Going back through the memory, it was almost euphoric as I floated above the trauma. I ran for my cell phone.

"Dr. Sue, I have to call and ask you this. That peace at the end … that isn't really possible. I don't remember anything beyond that point. I think I dissociated. Do you think I did? I felt myself leaving." The message I left was almost incoherent.

The answering call came quickly. "Yes, Janyne. I think you did dissociate. You stopped and opened your eyes and stared at me without blinking for probably two minutes."

This information placed high on my list of awkward moments. In my mind, I had stopped and opened my eyes and made eye contact for only a second before talking.

Now, like a form-fitting blanket, the coping strategy of

dissociation fell on top of several odd memories. Back in bed, my mind easily followed the path to floating. It felt euphoric. I could go there at will. Over the next few days it was difficult to stay in reality. I wondered, *Is this what happens when people "lose touch with reality?"*

It made sense that someone would choose to do this. My small-child self escaped by subconsciously removing herself from the pain. It was an effective coping mechanism for a helpless child; but was it the path my adult self should take for the rest of my life?

There Is More

Thus began a processing fury. I wondered how the little girl would have acted when she got back home. It was curious why I was able to stay with her through the trauma only to dissociate afterwards. What further memory could be worse? Was it why my parents called me difficult? More memories began to seep into my mind. As if moving on its own accord, my pen wrote, "There's more."

I stared at the words. A full-fledged panic attack engulfed me. With two days until my next therapy appointment, this was not a good sign. I tried to calm myself and then began stuffing random things in boxes—in a less than healthy attempt to stuff the memories back into my head. I needed to go back and stay with the little girl without dissociating. She needed someone to care about her.

After two very long days, in which a large portion of my house was furiously packed, I was once again in the waiting room. Panic rose inside me. Playing games on my phone did not help. My next step was clear but terrifying—for good reasons.

"Are you ready to return?"

"Yes, and no. It must be done, but I am afraid. Don't allow

me to dissociate. If I float, you need to send me back until what happened makes sense and the little girl knows someone cares."

I am in my bed. My stuffed animals are lined up around me. I am showing them where I hurt. I want them to care about what happened to me.

Suddenly, it was as if a tautly held slingshot was released. The memories rushed at me one after another. At first it seemed I was simply returning to the same memory time after time, but each one was slightly different....

He tells me, "It is a game we are playing. When I touch you it will feel good. I just want you to feel good, it won't hurt you. It is our little game. You don't want to tell anyone because then we can't play. They won't believe you. You will be in trouble. You don't want to be in trouble do you? See, I am not hurting you...."

"Now you are hurting me! You said you wouldn't. It never hurt before. Stop hurting me!"

He says, "Now be sure not to tell. No one will believe you."

I say to my parents, "I don't want to go back there. Please don't make me go back there."

But I was back again....

The playing is happening again. It isn't hurting. Now it is hurting!

"Wait, you said it wouldn't hurt. You are hurting me again. Oh, it hurts. Please don't make me hurt."

I am in bed. I still feel the pain deep inside of me. I am crying. I want someone to care that I am hurting. I have been sent to bed. I'm safe here, but I want someone to care.

I am crying, "No! I am not going back!" I am screaming, "No, I won't go back there. No, you can't make me go back there. I am not going. No! No! I won't go back." I can feel myself fighting with every bit of strength in my little body.

"You are embarrassing us. You are embarrassing us. These are good church people. What will they think if the minister's daughter throws this kind of fit and refuses to do what we tell her to do? You are embarrassing us."

I am in bed again. I am crying. I am wiping my tears on my stuffed puppy's ears. I hurt deep inside where I can't explain. But I did not go back.

My eyes opened and I felt where the pain had consumed me. My body had clearly told the story. The entire office building had probably heard my screaming.

Dr. Sue listened as I began processing.

"I was difficult and embarrassing. I asked not to go back, but was sent back anyway. When the pain happened again I decided asking for help was useless. I had to throw a fit so immense no one could force me to go. I *was* difficult."

"The church and the perfect front we presented to people was most important. My needs were subservient to our position in the church, and not embarrassing my mother became the Holy Grail. I had to find ways to live life and protect the damaged child inside of me. I protected myself."

"Yes, you did!" Dr. Sue said.

I sat reflecting on my words. I felt the small child was still watching me with her big blue eyes. She was led to trust and then was betrayed. It wasn't just the abuse; she was betrayed and thought no one cared. She needed someone to care, but asking was useless. She was destined to become a master at manipulating life in order to care for herself. She looked so small. This wasn't the end of the memories of the day this small child fought to not return, but it would be months before the remainder would surface. On this day, though, she was convinced someone cared.

The Impossible Task of Asking for Help

"What are you feeling, Janyne?"

"I honestly don't know. It wasn't just a one-time abuse. I was groomed and desensitized."

"Yes, you were. I am so sorry that happened to you."

"I was a target because of insecure attachment, wasn't I?"

"Yes, perpetrators look for those traits in children. Children with attachment issues are looking for attention, and it is easy to lead them. But you were strong. Yes, you were sent back once, but when it happened again you made sure they did not send you back a third time. You knew how to take care of yourself even when you were so little."

"I tried to get help. I asked not to go back, but it didn't work. I had to find a way not to be sent back."

"Yes, you were learning to take care of yourself."

"That is why I can't ask for help."

"But you have asked for help."

"Only after I put myself through days of torture."

"What do you think will happen if you ask for help?"

"I don't know exactly. There are so many levels. When I was little, it was just independence and wanting to do everything myself. When this happened, it turned into something more. If I ask for help and do not receive it … maybe it is rejection. No, the fear is that no one will care. I have to make sure people care about me. Asking is a sure way to find out they don't."

"But you know I care, right?"

Oh my goodness, yes. Could anyone have demonstrated care for me any more than this woman? I nodded.

"So, you will call if you need help?"

"Now that is hard. I am not sure I will call. It will send me to bed if I need help and have to ask."

"Let's make an appointment. I want you to come back."

"Yes, OK.... Whoa! Do you see that? I just got you to ask me to come back for another appointment without actually asking you."

"Yes, you did."

"I am really good at manipulation. I have practiced for almost my entire life. I need to ask you. I need to start learning to ask for help. Let me try it...."

I began. "I am afraid after what we found today and the chaos of my life, more help will be needed and I will end up in bed unable to ask for help. So, yes, can we please make an appointment?"

"Yes, we can," she said, smiling.

A Long Restless Night

My phone rang and upon seeing Dr. Sue's name a grateful sigh escaped me.

"Thank you for checking on me. It was a rough night. I'm rather disconnected today. You knew it would be rough, didn't you?"

"Yes, you did a lot of work yesterday. You had a lot to process. What was happening in the night?"

"I just kept waking up. There were dreams I wanted to exit, but I don't remember them. I was hurting as if I had truly experienced the pain. At one point I thought I was bleeding and actually went to the bathroom and checked before I was awake enough to think about it. I just can't function today. I keep shaking."

"The shaking is your body trying to release the trauma you held all these years. It's good you were processing this as you slept."

"There was just so much. It wasn't just an isolated incident. It's overwhelming to try to process. Unfortunately, I have to go masquerade as being normal today."

"Do you need to come in sooner than we planned?"

There it was—the war in me. "I just want to be well."

"You need to do this to be well. Can you come tomorrow?"

"I know it is what I need. Yes." My inner conflict with accepting the appointment was clear.

"Janyne, you can ask for help and you can accept it with a thank you when it is offered."

We both had to laugh at how simple it really was.

10
The Effects of Abuse

My child self could not have imagined someone would ever care this much. One day I would learn to care for myself, but it didn't appear it was going to happen anytime soon. In my defense, I had always taken care of myself—but with survival strategies. Giving up those strategies and learning new ways to care for myself would prove very challenging. My two-month trip to Seattle loomed on the horizon. Somehow, balance needed to be found!

What I did not realize was that part of the reason I could not stabilize was that child alters were standing in the wings, crying for help. I had difficulty understanding why my thought patterns and emotions kept dissolving in such childlike ways. I was doing all I could to try to find balance.

ONE MORE THING

Finding balance appeared to be completely outside of my grasp. One troubling aspect of the memory had not been addressed, and I was drowning in its wake. The feeling had been an unexplainable longing inside me. I knew this feeling had been a part of me for so long, it seemed like it was simply "me." I wrote the following (and more) to try to describe it:

If there is one thing that still stirs in me, it is the deep-seated need for "one more thing." I don't know what the

105

feeling is, but it probably came out of the abuse. I can't con-nect it to anything specific. It must be a trust issue, but it is part of the manipulation. If I can get this person to do this one more thing, then it will be clear they really care for me. This has been a struggle all through our journey.

I am driven by the need for someone to care. If a person will do "this one more thing" for me, then I will know they care. Asking is dangerous, though, because I don't trust they will say yes, and then in my mind it will be settled they don't care. This leaves me either waiting and hoping for one more thing or trying to manipulate it into happening. The other person doesn't even know I'm waiting for something to happen. Maybe I have no right to even want it. Maybe if they knew about my neediness, or if they realized they were being manipulated, they would reject me. So I must hide it. I end up feeling ungrateful for what people are doing for me, and that leaves me with guilt.

Oh, good Lord, I cannot control this need for "one more thing." I just want to go out and beat it to death.

Finally Finding Me

Since it wasn't possible to go out and beat this "one more thing" thinking to death, my brave self was going to have to take what I had written to therapy and set it in the middle of the room like a proverbial elephant. The pressure of trying to find balance before my upcoming trip probably drove me to this unprecedented level of bravery.

"I need to read you what I wrote. It is hard to read it."

"What are you feeling?"

"I never wanted you to see this 'me'."

"Explain more about this feeling."

"She is awful. She is dark. I have never let you see her. OK,

I am going to read what I wrote. I have to."

I felt like I'd jumped down the rabbit hole again.

My description of "one more thing" hung in the air between us. It made no sense. It wasn't logical. I finished and then in my attempt to explain it, the rambling began....

"You see, it is crazy thinking. I recognize crazy. I can see it in people immediately. I am like, 'Oh no ... you are not OK in your head. I must avoid you at all costs.' That is why I have hidden this 'me.' I don't want anyone to see her. People back away from crazy and needy, you know. I back away from it in others. I have worked my whole life to hide it—the darkness inside of me. I needed people to like me, to care for me; but if they saw this, they would leave me—walk away. I know what I should be like. I studied child development. I know what the research says I would be like, the issues I would have ... I was not ever going to let it happen to me. I did everything to cover it up so I would not be rejected."

With absolute calmness, Dr. Sue said, "We have some work to do. Shall we get started?"

My poor, confused brain was begging for help, but I had finally found "me" and it was all very confusing. I sat ready to begin EMDR, but surprisingly—even to myself—I crossed my arms and refused to begin.

"Are you ready?"

"No." Fear was gripping me tightly.

"What do you need?"

Holding my arms close to me, I sat staring at her. This was a first. I was just a never-ending surprise to myself. Slowly the words came from deep inside me.

"I am afraid now you have seen this darkness in me, you will think less of me. Do you think less of me?"

There it was.

"Oh, thank you for asking me. No! I do not think any less of you. You are hurting inside, and we need to help you."

Searching her eyes for the truth of her words, I found nothing to distrust. My arms slowly released their grip and with my hands on my knees we were ready to begin.

THE BLACK PUPPY

My eyes were closed, but everything in me was fighting.

"I am fighting it," I said.

There was a change in the rhythm of the EMDR tapping, which encouraged me to relax into the memory.

I am in my room. I see her on the bed crying. I think she is six. She is holding the black puppy. I feel her blocking me and pushing me away.

"The black puppy? I thought the puppy was white."

Oh, there are two. This is the one I hold when I am in the dark cloud. I still have this one in a box.

Oh my, I had kept so many things to help me to this day. This puppy was in the box with the white puppy. This black one made me very uncomfortable, so he had been left there. The long ears were in tatters—worn out with tears.

"What is she feeling?"

"I don't know. She doesn't know. There is blackness inside her that makes her cry."

The child began talking:

"You need to go talk to Jeannie. I am not talking to you. I don't talk to anyone. I don't know how you found me. Jeannie is the one you need to talk to."

There was another Jeannie off to the side who looked exactly like the one in the bed. Without any doubt there were two of them. They were distinct. I could feel them both, but the other Jeannie was a shadow. Maybe this little girl on the bed wiping her tears on the ears of the black puppy was the real one, but it felt confusing. There was nothing to do but talk to her.

"I am not leaving; I need to talk to you. I need you to know what happened to you—why you think you have blackness inside of you."

"Nothing happened to me. I am just black inside." She stared at me.

"No, it is not true. You were hurt; someone did something bad to you. You made yourself forget."

"No! That is not true! I am just dark inside."

"Come with me, let me show you."

I groaned. The only way to help her was to relive the memory. She sat with me as we felt the pleasure and then the searing pain. Now in the small girl's head, I felt the intense longing as she waited for the attention. This was the feeling from the previous session—wanting the attention, knowing maybe she shouldn't, but being unable to stop herself from wanting more.

"I wanted more."

The pile of tissues beside me was growing as the source of the longing became clear. There were no words to describe the longing. I was three years old again and had no words.

"I wanted this to happen to me." I heard the words come from deep inside me. "It felt good. I wanted more attention."

"Of course, you wanted attention," said Dr. Sue. "You

needed attention. You didn't want *this*. This was a bad person doing this to you. You were only three. You didn't know what was happening to you."

The pain began again. I felt myself lifting out of the room. I was floating again. The floating felt so good, but I forced myself back to the couch.

"I dissociated again."

"Did you leave her there?"

"Yes."

"We need to go back."

It was true. It would be a horrible weekend if I left her there. I now knew where the deep, conflicted longing for one more thing had begun. I knew my insecure attachment had made me a target. I also understood my little body had responded with pleasant sensations, which she had no way of understanding or explaining. I just wanted more. We needed to go back and help her.

"I am back in the room with the six year old. She is curled up on the bed crying. She has the black puppy."

"Can you talk to her?"

"I am going to curl up on the bed next to her."

"Good."

I began talking to the small, hurting child on the bed. "Do you remember now?"

"Yes, why did you make me remember?"

"You needed to know what the darkness was. It was someone who hurt you. It wasn't some awful thing inside you that you needed to hide. You were hurt."

She was crying, "Yes, it hurt. It still hurts."

It was true. Unexplainable abdominal pain had plagued me my entire childhood, but it was severe enough at about her age to keep me home from school. When I couldn't get out of bed, the pain was there—always.

I looked sadly at my child self. "You didn't do anything wrong."

"Yes, I did. I wanted more. I was waiting for more. I wanted it. It felt good until it hurt. I don't know why he hurt me."

"Yes, it did feel good. That wasn't wrong. He should not have been touching you, but it is not wrong for it to feel good. You were very little. You had no way of understanding any of this. You don't need to hide it anymore."

I looked intently into her eyes. I needed her to trust me. I needed her to believe my knowing would not make me reject her. I held her as she drifted away.

FINDING BALANCE ONCE AGAIN

"What are you feeling now?"

Dr. Sue watched me closely as I tried to form an answer.

"I am not exactly sure, but the illogical longing appears to be gone."

"Does this feel true?"

"Well, I'm going to have to test drive it, but maybe so."

We both laughed. The laughter was freeing. I could laugh again from my very core. I wasn't completely confident yet, but maybe it would be possible to become the person on the inside who others had always seen on the outside.

"Who goes to bed?" Dr. Sue always asked great questions.

It wasn't an easy answer because I had gone to bed so often. Maybe it was the six year old—overwhelmed by the brokenness inside her. She had no memory of what happened; she only knew she hurt inside—both physically and emotionally. She was crying without any ability to know why. She could remember the feeling, but couldn't connect it to anything. My mind was trying hard to understand everything.

"When I am in bed I am crying for help and can't help myself. Maybe I am the three year old when I am in bed."

"No, she couldn't help herself."

I continued rambling. "The floating at three—was it the first day this happened? I wouldn't have wanted to go back but maybe wasn't sure why? When it happened again, I think I remembered this time and threw the fit—but repressed the memory—and created Jeannie to live my life. So bed is my place to be three and float. I know I am dissociating. It feels like I am floating above my life. I have no words. I cry for help but am helpless to express it, because there is no memory of why I need to be there. I go there when life gets out of control and there is no way to care for myself."

"Yes, that makes sense."

"It makes sense for three; it is completely illogical for an adult woman." This made me laugh. It was a tragic laugh, but a laugh. My poor adult self had tried to live my life with the coping skills of a small frightened three year old!

"You know, my struggle about the attachment thing with you was very awkward but essential in order to get here. If it hadn't been staring me in the face all the time, I would not have read what I wrote about one more thing. It was so frustrating, I wanted to take it out and beat it to death. I think maybe we did."

Dr. Sue smiled. "Yes, but we couldn't put it on the floor and beat it. We had to find it inside of you and heal it."

"True, the unexplainable longing for one more thing makes sense now."

"What he took from you is so very sad."

I heard those words through the spinning replay in my head. There were so many ways this had affected me over the years. The shame and need to control were only the beginning. I had survived, but oh, the cost.

Maybe balance had been found once again. It was going to take me time to rebuild my life, value what had been accomplished, and figure out what the healed "me" needed and wanted to do with the rest of my life.

I was not evil inside. In fact, my journey was probably building an entirely new interpretation of the sin nature. The responsibility for adult choices was mine, but if control could have solved the problem, it would have been solved. The choices were need based and not the result of anything inherently evil in my soul. The needs were created when a very small child did not bond with her mother and then was sexually abused. Slowly, the lifelong effects of insecure attachment and early childhood sexual abuse began to mesh with everything I knew about child development. What happens to small children affects them for a lifetime.

LIFE JUST KEPT MOVING

Somehow in the midst of all the chaos of surfacing memories, the house was packed and preparations made for my dad's 100th birthday celebration. I spent days giving away possessions and packing what I didn't even know would be needed anymore. Soon relatives arrived from across the country and the condo filled with boxes, children, grandchildren, brothers and wives, cousins, one very old cat, and one crazy dog.

My dad's celebration could not have been any more perfect. The outpouring of love was overwhelming and the comfort of being with relatives was healing. In three days, the truck would be packed, and my daughter and grandchildren would be on their way. While packing to stay with them for two months, I desperately hoped the work I had done would help me remain functional.

The week was a blur and when the truck was packed and condo clean, I drove to the nursing home to say goodbye to my dad. In a state of exhaustion, I could barely get out of the car. The tenuous nature of life for someone who had just turned one hundred, weighed on me. It was possible this would be our last conversation. He was already in bed and peered at me in the dusk of the setting sun.

"Daddy, we are ready to go. I will be back in two months, but Scott will be back in a week."

"You need to go enjoy life. Travel. Enjoy your family."

He had given me the blessing. Back in my car, tears flowed freely while driving to a friend's house where I was to stay for the night. My car was full of things to unload, and she was helping me when her husband came outside.

She told her husband, "She hasn't said a complete sentence yet."

No, coherent thoughts were not possible.

We pulled out of town early the following morning. It was a three-day journey to my daughter's new life with her children. We unloaded the truck and began to establish a home out of the mass of boxes. Scott flew back to live with a friend and continue working.

It appeared I had found balance and there was hope that we had gotten to the final memory and simply needed time to heal. This felt true until the day I got lost while walking. Suddenly I was a six year old who didn't know how to use a GPS to find my way home. My hopes were dashed. It seemed one of the twins who spoke in the last memory had surfaced. The idea of shifting to small children was more than a little disturbing.

I called Dr. Sue.

She said, "Can you come back now? It appears there is more work to do."

No, the ticket was purchased and I had promised my adult children to stay and help them with their children and dogs. I had never been able to do this for them; but now retired, it was important for me to be there. So, I limped along with help from phone calls, emails, and long-distance appointments, as the children inside of me began to beg for attention. They had been patiently waiting for the adults to integrate and now they were demanding to tell their stories.

Part II
BROKEN

I almost wish I hadn't gone down that rabbit hole—and yet—and yet—it's rather curious, you know this sort of life! I do wonder what can have happened to me. When I used to read fairy tales, I fancied that kind of thing never happened, and now here I am in the middle of one!

—Alice

The second year of therapy was like falling down the rabbit hole yet again. This time, instead of finding three adults, I discovered children who often seemed to be playing a game of hide-and-seek. There was an infant, a three year old (and her imaginary friend), and twins who were born every year from six to ten. The theme was always "the one who lives" and "the one who holds the pain."

The continuing split identities appeared along developmental lines, but were most often caused by some form of trauma. It is hard to understand how trauma kept occurring despite my parents' best attempts to protect me—but it did. The horrible truth is that once a child has been abused, it is very likely it will happen again.

My inner life always has been in juxtaposition with my outer life because of the abuse. This was true as a child. My home life was not chaotic and, externally, I lived as any other child—but with odd behaviors. The same was true during the remainder of my life and was especially true during this year of healing children.

Outwardly, I was travelling, spending time with my children and grandchildren in the Seattle area, and living out my first year of retirement in an RV at the foot of the Rocky Mountains. Inwardly, I was working to heal a dozen children in hopes of integration. The only way to do this was to become the children, to allow them to live, share their stories, and to process the pain.

It felt as if I was Alice looking at my life from the other side of the looking glass. The fantasies of childhood had become my adult reality. I was Laura playing at Plum Creek, I spent weeks trying to help a small pilgrim free herself from her burden of sin, I felt the excitement of a child who thought she had finally found her Emerald City, and I searched endlessly to help an infant find a mother.

My willingness to embrace the children who had become fractured and frozen as a result of multiple traumas was the cornerstone to my healing process. By the time they began to surface, my acceptance of Jane opened the door to loving the small children who had helped me survive. Allowing myself to live within their developmentally frozen states has provided rare insights into the thoughts and emotions of traumatized children.

Much of what follows is taken from my writing during this time period. It is only a glimpse of what will be explored more fully in the sequel to this book. As I helped these children heal, I embraced their fantasies and told their stories with childlike whimsy, which at times cloaks the rawness of the trauma. My psyche was clearly processing in the only way it could—as a child. This is exactly how children survive trauma—by imagining worlds very unlike their own.

11
Setting the Stage

Working on this book became an integral part of my processing during the last months of therapy. Dr. Sue and I would meet and discuss what I had written and often stumble across intense emotions, which usually required additional therapy.

One day, as we sat reviewing what I had written in the children's section of this book, Dr. Sue pointed out that I was still avoiding feelings. It was perfectly acceptable for the children to write their stories in the way they did; but as an adult, I needed to not discount the emotional trauma they experienced and how difficult it was for me to heal each of them.

Try as I might to avoid what Dr. Sue was pointing out to me, it was true. How the children's section was written did not even begin to touch on the trauma my body had released in therapy. The trauma was held in my body and was released in very graphically physical ways during EMDR therapy and countless hours of shaking while I continued to process.

I was explaining it with my brain, but that was not where it was held. My body told the horrible truth of all that happened to me. *While cognitive talk therapy was part of the process, the true key to healing was the actual physical releasing of the trauma and the resulting shame.*

In EMDR therapy, the body releases and relives the trauma. It would have been easy to be frightened by the intensity of this process and back away before complete healing occurred. It is physical and intense, but it is also necessary to relive the trauma in order to release it from its frozen state and bring it to a place where it can be processed as an adult. This was essential to healing, because it allowed the physical pain and emotions of my small-child self to be released, felt, and processed.

When healed, the small children inside me began to tell their stories—in the delightful ways in which children should be able to tell their memories. The stories you find in the following section include their released memories, and the reader is left to infer much of the actual trauma involved in those memories. Their conversations were part of my processing and journeying toward integration. Their ability to tell the stories is an indication of true healing.

Since my intent was never to tell the details of the trauma, but instead to honor these small children who managed to find a way to live, I am completely satisfied with their storytelling. What is not adequately explained is the result of the trauma, which followed me throughout my adult life. It was not the traumatic event in and of itself that caused the most damage; it was the daily need to live above the pain in ways that would neither disrupt my life nor the life of my family.

After the release of the trauma involved in the stories told in this section, the truly difficult work of unwinding the psychological damage began. The ways in which I struggled with the brokenness of my three-year-old self every single day is truly beyond what I could have imagined. Her memories began surfacing early in therapy as she released the memory of her fear in the bathtub the day after she was abused. We returned to her again and again. The results of her trauma were embedded in my psyche in ways which were difficult to untangle and even more difficult to heal. I have added an addendum, "Childhood Trauma," at the end of this book, in which I more fully explain the profound effects of my insecure attachment and early childhood sexual abuse. It is essential for us to understand and help our youngest victims. I hope everyone will take time to read the addendum document!

Also, this entire section is storytelling in the sense that it did not surface in the tidy ways in which it has been written. The truth is here, and the reader is left to infer how I re-lived and processed these memories and traumatic experiences during EMDR therapy. Many traumatic memories processed during EMDR surface as fragmented pieces without linear form, but the true story falls in place during the subsequent "sense-making" processing. The writing here is my interpretation of the EMDR processed memory. The full story is not included, and the words neither explain how my body relived the horror nor how difficult it was to process between sessions. What is told here consumed my life for over a year.

Even as I wrote the final version of this section, in which I added the conversations I had with the children (and with God), my engagement with the children was part of my reality. It was in part due to my willingness to interact and care for these fragmented parts of my being that I have reached the place of wholeness in which I find myself today. Though children still pop up occasionally, they are a healed version of themselves and display the delightful characteristics held within the following true stories. Most of the time, they are simply part of the unique person known as Janyne.

Jeannie is the child heroine of this part of the story. She is brave and strong and taught the adult "me" how to live life against all odds. In my mind, she is the nine-year-old twin who found her voice. She is the Storyteller, and is usually my companion as I type. As the heroine, she acts as the spokesperson for all the children as they tell their stories.

How To Tell a Children's Story

"Wait!" It was Jeannie calling a halt to my typing.

I stopped typing, sensing her looking over my shoulder at my laptop. Her hands were, as usual, on her hips. She was clearly upset. "You told me you would not tell everything. Bad things happened to us and we never want you to tell some of them. You told us you wouldn't."

This was a concern we shared. "Sit here beside me, Jeannie. This is your story. If you do not want something to be told, it will never be told. There are young adult stories I chose not to tell and you will make this decision for the children. That's a promise!"

Jeannie looked at me for a long time before deciding to trust me (trust came slowly for this one). Then she said, "But they do need to know I wasn't difficult. I was almost always trying very, very hard to be good."

She was right. This small child, who managed to live despite what happened, needed to be honored for how hard she did try to be good. She always had a strong internal compass.

"No, you were not difficult. You were not a bad child. Bad things happened to you. I will be sure everyone understands this."

Jeannie smiled because Dr. Sue had often told her the same thing. She now appeared confident the story would be told the right way.

I asked, "Where should we begin?"

She grinned in her impish, endearing way and said, "At the beginning? But you said you would write another book just about us, so you don't want to tell everything, right?"

"Oh! Thank you, Jeannie. No, we just want to tell enough for everyone to understand why the young adult ended up on the cliff. Then we will write a book just about children."

We sat quietly side by side for a minute to consider what we needed to tell. It was complicated, because the children and their memories seemed to arrive in such haphazard ways. I wondered how Jeannie was going to be able to make sense of it.

It had taken months and layer upon layer to completely understand the entire child system. Each child had a unique role to play and a set of core memories—specifically of the trauma they had endured. They did not appear in order of their ages and sometimes one would actually hide another. In one case the entire system conspired to hide a particular child. It was a group of very clever and strong-willed children. Jeannie might have difficulty sorting it out.

"Jeannie, you are right, we just need to start from the beginning. We know the children didn't allow themselves to be seen in that order, but it might make more sense."

"Yes, we were hiding and didn't want you to find us until we were ready to tell our memories. Sometimes you almost saw one who wasn't ready and she had to run and hide. The only problem is, the children all have their own ideas about who should start first and they are getting kind of antsy."

Jeannie glanced behind her and I saw all the children in the midst of a discussion. Every single one of them was strong willed and opinionated. This was going to be interesting!

The Children Talk—All at Once

After a few minutes it seemed quite natural to Alice to find herself talking familiarly with them, as if she had known them all her life. Indeed, she had quite a long argument with the Lory, who at last turned sulky, and would only say, 'I'm older than you, and must know better.'

—Alice

"I need to go first," said the One Who Cries. "I am the one who figured out what to do with the pain."

Her twin, the One Who Lives, appeared to be skipping in and out of the group and not involved in the discussion.

"Well, maybe so," said the small Pilgrim, "but we were the ones who were always trying to figure out what the dark cloud was."

The Pilgrim's twin, the Problem Solver, nodded in agreement.

"If I hadn't taken care of all of you, you wouldn't be here to tell the story."

It was the Older Sibling—she was always in charge. Her twin, the Comforter, appeared to be trying to keep everyone calm.

"True, but I have been sitting and guarding the boards and holding the emotions back for a long time."

They all turned to look at the child with the hammer in her hand. There was now a board missing in the wall behind her, and what appeared to be dark oozing feelings were seeping out. The sight startled all of them since they had assumed the memories had all been healed. They quickly looked away and she scowled at them.

The one who looked just like her but was holding an empty box said, "Eventually, we have to talk about the Cave of Memories."

Everyone nodded in agreement.

"Wait, before any of you, there was me," said a very small voice. "I am the one who understands the dark cloud."

They all stopped and stared at her. She was so small, maybe three, and was holding a white, stuffed puppy. Her large blue eyes returned their gazes. They knew her eyes held pain, which should not be part of her young life.

"Let her begin. I have too much story to tell. Maybe I won't ever tell it."

Now they all turned to look at the one who spoke from the edge of the circle. There stood a nine-year-old with hands on her hips. Her eyes defied them to change her mind. She was right, she had the most pain, but she was also stronger. She was the one who always believed they would reach the Emerald City. They called her Nine. Her bike, Bluebird, was always right beside her. She was the Warrior who protected her sister, the Storyteller.

There was silence as they pondered all the sadness. They thought about Alice and how she almost drowned in her tears. They sympathized with her plight.

'I wish I hadn't cried so much!' said Alice, as she swam about, trying to find her way out. 'I shall be punished for it now, I suppose, by being drowned in my own tears.'
—Alice

There was a group shiver as they remembered how each of them almost drowned in their own tears while sitting on the couch. They weren't positive the crying was finished, but they believed telling the story would help—if they could just agree on who should start.

The Older Sibling who always sorted out their arguments stepped in.

"I am the oldest and can make this decision. It only makes sense to tell the story from the beginning. We have to begin with the Baby. We can help her with the words."

12
Early Childhood Years

When trauma occurs during the first few years of life, the trauma will most likely be buried in what psychologists call infantile or childhood amnesia. This in no way indicates the memories are gone. Trauma hides the memories in fragmented pieces in the child's developing mind, but the emotional effects remain for a lifetime.[1]

My earliest memories, which had always seemed nonthreatening, all proved to be trauma related. These early memories included standing by a gate holding a doll, a front yard with toys and a chain-link fence, a grey darkness in a room with linoleum tiles, a green room with windows, and crying on a crinkly bed while wiping my tears on my white puppy's ears. These seemingly random memory fragments did not appear to be connected, but they were.

---

1. It is the primitive limbic brain that holds the earliest experiences with all the emotions and the meaning of each memory, as they were experienced. During EMDR therapy pre-verbal /pre-cognition experiences can be retrieved from the limbic brain which holds the earliest fight-or-flight protective responses. The effects of trauma wind their way into the personality in a myriad of ways—without any memory of why.

The Youngest Speaks

'Speak English!' said the Eaglet. 'I don't know the meaning of half those long words, and, what's more, I don't believe you do either!'

—Alice

Jeannie was concerned. When concerned, she often talked to God. "God, you know when Baby tells her story, not everyone will believe we can know what happened there. They won't understand how EMDR helped us remember things we had hidden even from ourselves."

God sighed. "Some believe they know everything. They think they can explain me. Job tried to do that. Do you remember what I said? 'Have you comprehended the vast expanses of the earth? Tell me if you know all this.' Man cannot even comprehend the vast expanses of the earth, or the universe—certainly not the human brain. This is your story to tell. I have loved you from the womb, and I know the truth of what Baby will tell."

Jeannie, looking satisfied with God's answer, turned to the very small child.

"Baby, tell us what you remembered during EMDR. We believe you."

"I can see through the rails. I am in my crib. I can hear talking, but it is far away. I want someone to come pick me up. I am waiting. I don't fuss. I look around and see the light coming in the window. Something sparkles in the light and I like to watch it.

"There she is! I am learning to smile and I smile at her, but she never looks at me. She is putting a dress on me. I can feel how soft it is. Oh, she is bending my arm to make

it go into the dress. I don't like how she does it. I try to explain, but she isn't listening, because I can't talk. I hear talking. She is gone. I see someone looking over the edge of the rails. It is my brother. He looks at me and talks to me, but then he is gone. She is there again. I try to get her to look at me and pick me up, but she doesn't. She acts like she is going to, but she sets me on a pillow and I hear a click. I am smiling at her, but she won't look at me.

"I am older—two. They said my brother was at a hospital. Daddy is carrying him into the house. He looks upset. He is in bed, and they are doing something to him under the sheet. He looks so unhappy. My mother sees me and tells me to leave and shuts the door. I am afraid. Why can't he walk? I am in my bed crying. My other brother is pulling my hair and asking why I am crying. I am afraid. What were they doing to him? Why did someone hurt him?

"I am older—maybe three. I am at a gate. I am holding my doll. I am not going in the gate. No! I won't go in the gate. No, you can't make me go in the gate."

And with that, like the mouse telling his story to Alice, the baby who was now three stopped.

'Please come back, and finish your story!' Alice called after it. And the others all joined in chorus. 'Yes, please do!' But the Mouse only shook its head impatiently and walked a little quicker.
                                                              –Alice

The Baby refused to continue. They all understood how sad she was about not having a mother who would look at her. They decided the adults had explained enough about how this had affected all of them. She was always trying to understand everything because she was very smart, but no one thought she needed an explanation as to why adults did things to children under sheets and blankets. No more needed to be said, so it was decided to let the next child begin.

When I Was Three

Everyone looked at the small three year old and waited for her to talk. But she ignored them and sat on the floor playing with her blocks.

"Do you want to tell your story?"

She looked up at Jeannie with her big blue eyes. "You mean what happened behind the gate? I already told about it."

"But there was more, wasn't there? It was a long time before you told the rest of your memory. In fact, you hid it so well that we almost never got to hear it. I understand why you didn't want to tell. It was sad; but what happened after that is very, very important."

She sighed and stood up.

The adult me pulled her into my lap. "You are safe here. Would you like me to tell the story and you can help me?"

She nodded yes.

The ten-year-old Comforter walked toward me as small Jeannie snuggled into my lap. In her hands she held the white, stuffed puppy. "Here, Jeannie. This will help you while we tell the story. You don't have to be afraid anymore."

The small, three-year-old Jeannie looked grateful and held the puppy tightly.

The Green Room with Windows

One of my most haunting memories was of lying on a crinkly bed in a glowing green room. I was crying and wiping my tears on the ears of a small white stuffed puppy. There were windows with blinds pulled partially closed and people were walking up and down a hallway outside the door. I was alone.

Jeannie looked up at me and said, "We told about the green room and Dr. Sue helped us."

"Yes, do you want me to tell what you remembered?" She nodded yes....

"I am on the bed crying. My mother and father are here. My mother is upset. I hear her talking. 'She has to stop crying. I can't stay in this room if she keeps crying.' I am trying to stop, but I can't. She is leaving. My daddy is looking at me. 'Jeannie, I need to go take care of your mother. I need you to be brave.' I am being very strong and brave, but I can't stop crying.

"The door opens. It isn't my daddy. It is a man and a woman. He has a white coat on. She is all in white. She was the one we followed down the hall to the room. She has white shoes that go scrunch scrunch and a tiny white hat on her head. 'Hello, Jeannie. I'm the doctor. You're safe here, but I need to take off your panties and see if you are hurt. I won't hurt you. I want to help you feel better.'

"I know what is going to happen. I am up in the air looking down. I see them looking at my panties. It looks like I pooped in them, but I am a big girl. I don't poop in my underwear. They are looking at each other and shaking their heads. The doctor is walking to the door. Daddy is in the hall with my mother. He asks them to come in. But she won't come in. So they stand in the doorway. I hear them.

"'Rev. Jenkins, I am sorry, but something very bad happened to your daughter today. Where was she today?'

"My mother is upset. 'She was with a good family from our church today. That did not happen.' She walks away down the long hallway. Her heels go clip clop, clip clop.

"The doctor is talking to Daddy. 'You should call the

police, but it is your choice. She is so small; she probably won't remember what happened today. We can give her something to sedate her, so you can take her home.'

"Daddy is helping me sit up. He's telling me to drink something. It's icky sweet. He's wrapping me in a blanket with my puppy. He's picking me up to carry me.

"He is walking down the long hallway. I feel sleepy and stop crying. The lights flash into my eyes as we walk under them. We are at the car. He is laying me in the back seat.

"My mother is upset because they can't take me back to that place, and she keeps saying it didn't happen. My daddy is trying to talk in whispers to her. I'm too sleepy to stay awake."

The small version of Jeannie in my lap seemed so small. She was holding the puppy tight and sucking on two middle fingers, but she pulled them out of her mouth long enough to say, "My daddy took care of me and helped me stop crying. I fell asleep. Dr. Sue was sad when we told her this."

"Yes, Jeannie, she was sad and understood why we all kept telling her we thought she would walk away from us. She told us she would never walk away. She kept her promise, didn't she?"

"Yes, she always took care of us and kept her promises."

Jeannie looked up at me. "But the green room wasn't the worst part, was it?"

No, it wasn't. I didn't want her to have to tell the rest, but what happened after that day wouldn't make sense without it.

Jeannie tried to look brave. "It's OK; you can write what I remembered."

Slowly sliding back to how the memory surfaced during therapy, I began to type....

"I am rubbing the sleep out of my eyes. The light is coming in the Venetian blinds and I can see the dust in the rays of light. The wires from the top bunk are above me. I can't move. I am afraid. I can't move! A rough blanket is around me. It is from the green room. It is tight and I can't get my feet loose. I have to go potty! I am yelling, but no one is coming, and I can't stop it. I am crying.

"My mother is here now. 'Why are you crying?' I couldn't get out of the blanket and I had to go potty. She is angry. She is unwrapping me. 'Look, the mattress is wet. Go to the bathroom and take off your clothes and wait for me.' I am running out the door. I don't have my underwear on.

"I'm sitting on the toilet and waiting. She is pouring the water and telling me to get in. I'm in the water, but something is floating in the water around me—it is red. I don't know what it is. I scream for her to get me out. Scream and scream! I try to get out.

"'Get back in the tub! You are dirty, you are dirty, you are dirty.'

"I'm crying. I don't want to get back in with the red.

"'Stop crying. Wash yourself off and here is a towel and your clothes.' Why isn't she helping me? She always helped me. Whoa! I slip getting out. I am crying. I try to dry myself. The clothes are hard to put on because I am wet. I am not dry enough. I am in my room. My sheets are gone, and I can't find puppy. I find my doll. I curl up in the corner. I am rocking and rocking and rocking."

Feeling the couch underneath me again, I realized my body was rocking and it appeared Jeannie had fallen asleep. She held so many emotional triggers! There was the fear of someone walking away from me. My dislike of taking a bath or cleaning bathtubs now made sense. I always slept lightly and got up to use the restroom multiple times in a night. Putting on clothes when wet sent me into a toddler meltdown. I found it very unsettling to sleep in a sleeping bag or have my feet constrained. My worst nightmares involved waking up paralyzed and unable to move. On the bright side, warm hospital blankets always comforted me.

It was good Jeannie had fallen asleep. My arms were tightly wrapped around her. Her memory in the bathtub had surfaced very early in therapy, but we could not connect it to anything. I just kept screaming for someone to get me out. Dr. Sue told me she wanted to get a towel, wrap me in it, and hold me. We couldn't understand why no one came to help me or why the memory held such obvious trauma.

JEANNIE CRIES FOR DADDY

Small Jeannie had been sleeping through months of therapy and beyond. Then suddenly she awoke and said she needed Dr. Sue. Where she took us was unexpected.

"What do you need to tell her, Jeannie?" I asked her.
"I want to thank her for taking care of me. I want to tell her what I could never tell my mother," she answered.

This seemed like an odd kind of surfacing, but it took us back to the couch where her still unresolved pain became evident.

Dr. Sue said, "We need to work with this feeling."

Instead of a specific memory, in EMDR it seemed like a black fog. It seemed that I was drowning under indescribable emotions.

I screamed, "I hate you! I hate you! I hate you!"

Something was erupting. In two years of therapy we had

never seen anything quite like it. What was left was a desolate peace. For days I pondered the meaning of what had been dislodged.

> *Small Jeannie appeared again. "Thank you for taking me to Dr. Sue." Her sad blue eyes looked at me.*
>
> *"You were the one screaming? You were asleep in the corner. You were shaking and rocking. I thought you had gone to sleep and were OK. I am sorry you were left there. You were right to ask to go see her again."*
>
> *"I screamed at my mother. I shouldn't have said that."*
>
> *"Oh, my! Your emotions are what exploded out of me! It was you. You were frightened, and she had been awful to you. You had every reason to hate her."*
>
> *I felt the deadness inside of this small child. This deep sense of deadness had always been part of me. It was as if she did not want to exist. Was it possible for a small child to feel annihilation? "Jeannie, do we need Dr. Sue again?"*
>
> *"Yes."*

Back on the couch, there were no words to explain the deadness inside of me. It felt like loneliness, but worse—complete aloneness. Somehow, what had been released in the previous session had left this deadness exposed.

> *"I am in my bed, crying. We just moved. I am ten and so lonely. There are no friends. No one at this church loves and cares for me…. I am older—in high school. There are no friends again. Loneliness … awful loneliness. I am sitting in the corner rocking. I have a doll because I can't find my puppy. She isn't soft like my puppy. Rocking, rocking, rocking. 'Where is my daddy? I want my daddy!'"*

The intense feelings of this child inside of me were

overwhelming. She needed her daddy, but he had to go to the church.

Tears poured out of her eyes and onto my cheeks. Her mother had rejected her, the man she trusted had hurt her, and her daddy had gone to church and left her with the mother who thought she was dirty. The depth of deadness in her small soul seemed impossible for such a young child.

Through my sadness, I heard Dr. Sue asking, "Can you go to her and wrap her in a blanket?"

"I am looking for a blanket. I look on the bed, but there isn't one. I look in the linen closet, but they don't seem right. I need to go to the hospital and get a warm blanket. She loved the warm blanket she was wrapped in. I am on the floor next to her. I am wrapping it around her and pulling her into my lap and rocking her. She can't stop crying and shaking. There are not enough tears to take away the deadness inside of her. I keep rocking and rocking and rocking while she cries. She is sleeping again."

She needed me to take care of her. I left therapy that day knowing my job for the next few days was going to be to hold my three-year-old self.

"Jeannie, I will come and bring warm blankets whenever you are sad. You can cry and cry until you don't need to cry anymore. Hating your mother and screaming those words at her was completely understandable. She should have loved you. She should have held you. I don't know why she couldn't. But you won't need to scream at her anymore, because I am holding you."

Wrapping her tightly and kissing her on the forehead, I kept rocking until she began snoring as she sucked on her two middle fingers. Would it be possible to heal the deadness and fill it with love? I would have to figure it out, but first she needed to rest and cry the pain away. We would need a lot of warm blankets.

> *Waking again, she said, "When I yelled at her, she left and slammed the door. It was getting dark when Daddy came and found me in the corner and picked me up. She said I screamed at her. He told her to make my bed, and he tucked me in. I always wanted someone to tuck me in bed and kiss me on the forehead. I wanted someone to care."*
>
> *"Jeannie, you have been trying to tell me this about being kissed on the forehead. I didn't understand. It seemed like something we wanted to be true, but I wasn't sure it was. I had found so many cover stories created to hide the true trauma. I was afraid this was another one. I am sorry I didn't believe you."*
>
> *She looked at me with her most serious look and said, "Yes, you should have believed me. I was sad. I needed to be kissed on the forehead like you are doing now."*

After Jeannie told what happened that afternoon, many rough days of processing followed. Suddenly, I was three years old and experiencing outbursts, uncontrollable shaking, and inability to make myself do even the simplest tasks. Jeannie was in the fore.

Something was wrong—Scott knew it, I knew it, Dr. Sue knew it.

> *Jeannie seemed to be trusting me at first; then one day as I tried to wrap her in a blanket, she pushed me away. "Will you talk with Dr. Sue about this? Is there more? Will you tell her everything?"*
>
> *She looked angry and afraid but nodded yes.*

She appeared completely exhausted from holding something too tightly inside her.

Glimpses kept seeping, but it felt important to wait for help. I sat in bed unable to move and buried myself in blankets to keep from shaking. The afternoon was eternal. It was discouraging to find myself in a place where I needed rescuing again. I thought those days were behind me, but apparently my three-year-old self had not fully healed.

JEANNIE TOLD US MORE

Desperately wanting what Jeannie had told me about my dad rescuing her to be true—but doubting it at the same time—I returned to the couch. My adult frustration was evident.

"I am not frustrated with a three year old. I am frustrated with the adult me not being able to take care of her."

I told how this small child had begun to push me away and realized she didn't think her memory had been believed. Not believing myself was never a good idea.

"Shall we go see if we can help her?"

I nodded yes.

"I can see her sitting on the floor still. She is crying and shaking. I am sitting next to her. I am shaking now. I am crying and shaking. I can hear my mother walking around the house. Sometimes she clip clops on the hardwood floors, sometimes she is on carpet. I hear her coming to the door. The door is opening.

"'No! I hate you! I hate you!'

"She is yelling at me, 'Don't you ever say that. Never say that to me again. You need to come eat your lunch.' I don't

want to go. I am not hungry. She is angry because I won't come. She is pinching my arm with her fingernails. I am crying, 'Please don't hurt me. I'm not hungry.' But I am in the kitchen at the little table. I am pushing food around the plate. 'Eat your food. Stop playing.' I am trying to eat. Oh no! I am going to throw up. I am crying, the throw up is all over my plate and the table.

"'You made yourself throw up again, didn't you?' No! 'Go to the bathroom.' I don't want to be put in the tub again. I am crying and shaking. I don't have any choice. I can clean up fast. My clothes are there. I can't get dry but I get my clothes on. I am back in the corner. I can't stop shaking, crying. I want to go to sleep … the door is opening. 'No! Don't come in here!' It is my daddy. 'Jeannie, why are you on the floor? It is OK. Why aren't you in bed?' I am crying. 'There are no sheets on my bed. I went potty in the bed. I got my bed wet. I can't find my puppy.'

"He is talking to my mother, 'Go get the sheets. Why didn't you make her bed?' She is answering, 'They were wet and had to be hung on the line and every time I came in here she screamed at me.' She is making the bed. Daddy is holding me. He is asking about my puppy. 'It was filthy. I washed it. It is still wet.' He is telling her to go get my puppy. He is tucking me in bed and giving me the icky medicine. I can smell the sheets have been on the clothesline.

"'This will help you, Jeannie. Look, here is your puppy where you can see him. He is still too wet to get in bed with you, but you can see him. The medicine will help you go to sleep. I need to go talk to your mother, but you can go to sleep now.' He is kissing me on the forehead. I am looking at my puppy. I want him in bed with me, but I can tell he is still wet.

"I hear loud talking. 'Why didn't you make the bed and put her in?' 'She kept yelling at me every time I went in. She threw up her lunch.' My daddy sounds upset. 'She is a child. You are her mother. You need to take care of her. Do you understand what happened to her?' Mommy is upset too. 'Yes, she was ruined.' No one is talking. Daddy is talking. 'You will never say that about her again, never again.' I am very sleepy. Ruined. That is what happens when I tear my tights. She says they are ruined. She throws them in the trash … I am so sleepy."

At this point I was holding the small three year old, thankful the medicine was helping her sleep. She had meant there was more to the memory, but everything she had said was true. She had just tried to leave out some of the awful parts—a skill at which my child self became adept.

Everyone was watching her as she slept. We just wanted her to sleep the deep sleep that she had never experienced from that day forward. The night terrors were ahead of her. There was more to her story, but it wasn't safe for her to tell more now. The others would help her tell the rest in the children's book. She had told enough for today. Everyone understood how what happened that day would eventually lead to the cliff.

13
Early Elementary Years

'Come, there is no use crying like that!' said Alice to herself rather sharply. 'I advise you to leave off this minute.' She generally gave herself very good advice (though she very seldom followed it), and sometimes she scolded herself so severely as to bring tears into her eyes; and once she remembered trying to box her own ears for having cheated herself in a game of croquet she was playing against herself, for this curious child was very fond of pretending to be two people.

–Alice

Yes, like Alice, I was fond of being two people. While I am not exactly sure how old I was when the first split occurred, there was a fascinating EMDR therapy session in which I was unable to contain the tension building inside of me. As the tension exploded, it appeared to divide into good and bad feelings, memories, and emotions. While this processing is not completely clear, what had been a three year old and her imaginary friend (in the form of puppy) appeared to now be The Watcher (Gatekeeper) and twins approximately six years old.

The children had chosen not to tell about the abuse that occurred, despite my parents' best efforts at protection, when I was six. Layers of triggers were resolved while working through this memory, one being the great difficulty of feeling trapped in a house on a snowy day. I am thankful to know the source of this; now I can acknowledge this child's fear and still enjoy a cozy day inside.

The next set of twins appeared to be seven: the Girl with the Hammer and the Girl in the Cave of Memories. These two children were extremely sensitive and doing their very best to process increasingly difficult memories.

It is unclear what created the final twins during this time period, but twins approximately eight years old played important roles in my spiritual development as they tried to understand the dark cloud. I called them the Pilgrim and the Problem Solver.

These six children were delightfully different from each other. To me this is an indicator of the challenges in forming a clear sense of self during these developmentally important years. I treasure their uniqueness and their personalities are embedded in me. Their stories surfaced as a result of EMDR therapy, and these children are perfectly happy to have them told through selected samplings of my process writing. The first selection is an extension of the twin story that emerged during the summer between the first and second year of therapy.

THE ONE WHO CRIES IN THE BED

"Why are you crying?" I asked the small child in the bed.

"You're not supposed to talk to me," she said. "Talk to her. She's the one who goes out and lives." She pointed across the room to another child. They both looked like the same six-year-old Jeannie, but there were two of them.

"I need to know why you are crying."

"Because it is my job. I am the One Who Cries. She is the One Who Lives."

"Well then, what are you crying about?"

"I don't know." She hugged her puppy more closely and wiped her tears on his ears.

"Well, can you explain why there are two of you?" I felt somewhat like Alice stepping through the looking glass.

"You have to talk to her." She pointed again to the other seemingly identical child.

I turned once again to the other child. "She said to ask you why there are two of you."

"Simple. I am the one who goes out and lives. If something bad happens, I come back and hand it to her, and she cries about it, so I can keep playing."

"Doesn't that seem just a bit unfair to her?"

"No; how silly that is. It is her job. She was created to cry. She cries in the bed. I was created to live. How could I go have fun if I needed to stop and cry all the time?"

There certainly was logic in what she was saying, but my question remained unanswered.

"Do you know why she is crying?"

"No! Knowing would make me sad, wouldn't it? I can't play if I am sad."

The logic was complete. It appeared neither one knew why the One Who Cries was crying. This was not going anywhere. They were quite comfortable in their dual roles. Maybe learning more about them would help.

"Can you tell me about yourself?" I asked.

"I am Jeannie and I am six. I like to play outside mostly. I have a mother, father, and two brothers. I go to school and we all go to church where my daddy is a preacher. My mother is a teacher. We live in Albuquerque. My daddy taught us how to spell it. A.L.B.U.Q.U.E.R.Q.U.E."

Beaming with pride, she continued. "Our favorite thing

to do is to go to eat at Old Town on Sunday after church. I can watch them make sopapillas. You pour honey in them and they are my favorite things to eat. I get to put sugar in my milk. I am learning to read, but am not very good at it yet. My big brother is sixteen and hangs out with his friends and doesn't want me to tag along. My other brother and I fight sometimes. I like to play in the empty lot behind our house, but I am not supposed to go in the arroyo. There are lots of kids to play with. I like to go to church. Everyone likes me there. Mr. Counts always gives me candy."

It sounded like a good life for a little girl; I wondered why her sister would need to cry in the bed.

"So, what makes you sad?"

"You don't understand. I am not sad, she is." Again, she pointed to the one in the bed, who yes, was still crying.

I noticed she hadn't said much about her mother. "So, tell me more about your mother."

"No! Now you need to go talk to her," she said, and immediately she left the room to go play.

Walking over to the child on the bed, I asked if I could sit down beside her. She nodded her head and moved to the side.

"Do you cry because of your mother?"

"Maybe so. When my sister brings me things to be sad about, it is usually about my mother, but there are other reasons."

"Why does your mother make you cry?"

"She doesn't love me."

"Are you sure? I know it is how you feel, but what makes you so sure she doesn't love you?"

"Well, we watch other mothers and they talk to their

children and hug them and hold them when they are afraid. Our mother doesn't do any of those things, so we are sure she doesn't love us."

With this proclamation, she returned to the crying, and I saw no need to press her any further. There had to be something more, but she certainly didn't seem to remember anything—at least not anything she was ready to share at this time.

EMBRACING TWINS

Both twins were watching as I wrote. The One Who Lives began talking, "We like that story. It makes us smile because you were so confused when you saw two of us. Thank you for helping us remember why my sister was crying. We feel better now."

With that pronouncement, they grabbed each other's hands and ran to play as one child. The remainder of their story would wait.

The full story of the twin six year olds, which included additional abuse in situations where I should have been safe, surfaced over a yearlong period, but I first saw them at the end of the Three Chairs phase of therapy when the One Who Cries thought there was darkness inside of her. Even after helping them understand the abuse, their struggles with my mother were never ending.

My time with these twins will probably always be my favorite part of the healing journey. Returning from Seattle, we had an opportunity to purchase a fifth-wheel trailer and move into Garden of the Gods RV Resort. A creek ran alongside the property, and the entire area could have been where I went to the creek as a child. These twin children relived their childhood in this place. We spent time at the creek, throwing sticks into the current and collecting rocks. I ran down the creek chasing the sticks and had many conversations with God as the sun shone through the golden leaves of fall. The creek was a place of healing.

These two began my journey of learning how to love and embrace the small children inside of me. As they began to heal and integrate, I feared losing them; but in truth, they never left. As the memories healed, I was no longer triggered to shift and be a child. The shifting was the result of unresolved pain. The process of healing the pain was long and complicated. As shifting lessened, it made being an adult infinitely easier, but I never wanted to lose the essence of these two children who lived inside of me. In a sense, there was a grieving process as they became less distinct from each other, but they are still very much a part of me. The One Who Cries helps me when I need to ride the waves of feelings. The One Who Lives is my little Explorer who always wants to see what is around the next corner.

A Hammer, Lots of Boards and Boxes, and a Cave

Two more identical children stood in front of me. They appeared a bit older than the first two twins—probably seven. Beside one was a pile of boards, and in her hand was a hammer. The other child held a box, which was well worn and empty. Behind them a path ended at the entrance to a cave. There were more boards on the ground outside the cave, and inside the cave were piles of opened empty boxes. The two children looked sad.

"Hello, Sevens! Why are we looking so sad today?"
The one with the hammer in her hand spoke, "We always knew what our jobs were. We had important jobs and now you don't need us anymore."

"Oh! No wonder you look sad! Let's talk about how important those jobs were and then we will work on a solution to this problem."

The look of pride returned to their faces, and the one with the hammer looked at her twin and urged her to go first.

"My job was to take the bad memories and feelings and put them in boxes inside the Cave of Memories. I organized them on the shelves she built for me." She was looking at her sister in awe because she could build anything, just like Daddy.

What she had done was amazing.

"It was a very important job! We would not have survived if you hadn't taken all those bad memories and boxed them up. Besides, you were so organized! When we needed a memory, you knew exactly where to find it. You even told me what things to keep in the boxes I carried around."

She beamed with pride as her sister began talking.

"Well, sometimes the bad feelings oozed out of the boxes and tried to get out of the cave. So we decided I should board up the entrance to keep them there. See all the boards?"

I could see all the boards now littering the ground. What she had done was impressive.

"Your job was so important! You kept the feelings from oozing out and drowning me! We couldn't have survived without you either!"

Now they were both beaming with pride, but suddenly they were sad again. I understood and needed to help them.

"Listen, you were so brave when you began to tell us the memories."

Looking at the one holding the hammer, I said,

"Remember the day Dr. Sue asked you to pull a board down." Both girls shuddered. *"Yes, you were afraid the oozing would begin, but by that time we had healed so many memories, it really wasn't as bad as we thought it would be, was it?"*

They both shook their heads in a united, *"No."*

"It seems the problem was this.... You two were busy with these jobs and never got to do the things you would have enjoyed doing. You were seven! You should not have had to do these jobs. You should have been playing. Keeping the memories contained made you both so anxious we all thought we might drown in the anxiety. You should not have had to live in fear of emotions. You are much more than these jobs. While you were healing, I learned a lot about you."

The two looked slightly curious.

"It was sometimes hard to tell you apart because you are so much alike. You were the children who listened to the classical music records to soothe yourselves. You both loved to be alone—especially to sit in our favorite chair and draw. You were my little organizers and you loved to watch Daddy build. You also liked to be outside and hear the birds and crickets. You were the ones who got to go to Sandia Peak, and you loved the lights of Albuquerque when we came over the hill. You love quietness, snow, Christmas, and gentle, soft feelings."

They were smiling at me and appeared to be merging in and out of each other. They were so close to being only one child, and they were an essential part of me. They helped me be content with the very simplest of things. They were the part that begged to go on solitary picnics, drive through Garden of the Gods while listening to classical music, and watch the snow fall while working a jigsaw puzzle.

"What do you two (or is it one) think your new jobs should be?"

"Well, we had a hard time understanding feelings. Remember our journal where we wrote and drew about feelings when we went to San Diego?"

"Oh yes! You helped me so much! We had so much fun finding feelings! None of us could tell them apart from each other. We had to look up definitions."

"Yes we liked that. Can we keep drawing feelings? And can we help you find more ways to enjoy simple things? We love simple things. We are so glad the anxiety is better. Thank you for helping us!"

"Absolutely, and yes, we will get out the journal again. Do you understand why we couldn't tell the difference between the emotions?"

They shook their heads no.

I looked at them sadly; the feelings had been processed but not explained to them.

"You know bad things happened to you and the other twins, right?"

They nodded their heads yes.

"Well, because of what happened, everything made you afraid—even good things. Feelings got all wound up together and made you anxious about every little thing. You didn't have anyone helping you understand when you got upset. You just began to put everything in boxes and hid the boxes in the Cave of Memories."

The one with the hammer began speaking. "We didn't have to be afraid of everything did we? We had bad dreams about moths in our bed. It wasn't really about moths was it? We were afraid of moths, but they didn't ever hurt us."

"No, you see, everything reminded you of the bad things.

You were afraid of everything until your sister began putting your fears in boxes. It was a very smart plan! She kept it so organized. When we needed a memory, it was easy to find! But you two do not need to do that anymore. We can keep memories, but they are healed and no longer ooze out of the boxes. We don't need to be afraid of them anymore."

The twins smiled and, suddenly, we were all in a gentle hug and the cave and boards began to vanish leaving the beautiful path in front of us.

I wondered if they might want to tell something more about their stories, but upon asking, they said, "No, you can tell more about us in the other children's book."

"Shall we walk?" I asked. The two started skipping ahead to see what they could find to show me. Sometimes they were two, but mostly they were one and when my soul longs for quiet pursuits I go looking for them.

THE SMALL PILGRIM

I, your dear friend, am in myself undone by reason of a burden that lieth hard upon me...

–Christian

I recognized her immediately—eight years old, chin set, pigtails flying. The look in her eyes was one of complete determination. There were two, but they seemed much more of a team than the six year olds. (The seven-year-old twins were still hiding.) These two appeared to be on a mission. One was living and the other was thinking—a lot—because she had a problem. She had heard about the Story Lady and she was determined to get her sister to go hear *Pilgrim's Progress*!

"Can I come to hear the story? Please! I will be very good.

I know it is for the older children, but I promise you will not even know I am there!"

This small eight year old was very persistent and convincing. She was at the campground and had seen the sign stating that every afternoon during campmeeting the Story Lady would be telling the story of Pilgrim's Progress with flannelgraph. She wanted to hear the story—very much.

It was the first day and she was eagerly waiting on the stairs. She was early. She didn't want to miss anything. Then she was sitting at the edge of her chair—it was precarious, because the wooden folding chairs often collapsed unexpectedly if one wasn't careful. She didn't seem to be concerned about it. She was watching the Story Lady— and the flannelgraph piece of Christian with a terrible burden on his back.

"My twin has a burden just like the one he has," she thought.

Her twin's burden was more like a dark cloud hovering over her, but it looked so much the same. She felt like she was dragging it around with her all of the time. She was here to listen to the story, but maybe she could help her sister. She began to listen even more intently.

"Wait! The Story Lady is talking about Evangelist. I know evangelists. They come to tell us about Jesus. He is helping Christian."

When the day's section of the story ended, she still did not know what the burden was. Evangelist told Christian to go to the Wicked Gate, but the story ended. She would have to come back to find out what happened. (Much later in life she would learn it was a wicker gate—though considering the dark cloud, "wicked" made perfect sense.)

Oh her despair when the Story Lady could not come and

she had to wait another day. She so wanted to learn what the burden was!

This miry slough is such a place as cannot be mended; it is the descent whither the scum and filth that attends conviction for sin doth continually run, and therefore it is called the Slough of Despond; for still, as the sinner is awakened about his lost condition, there ariseth in his soul many fears, and doubts, and discouraging apprehensions, which all of them get together, and settle in this place. And this is the reason of the badness of this ground.

—Pilgrim's Progress

There it was. The Story Lady had explained the burden on Christian's back was sin. It was the bad things he had done.

"Well," she thought, "I have done bad things. I am always in trouble for one thing or another. Mother is always upset with me. The dark cloud must be sin. It makes my sister feel like she is drowning just like Christian was in the slough!"

This small child had her first answer. She was a Pilgrim in search of how to be rid of the awful dark cloud of sin. She would keep coming until she found out how to be rid of the awful thing!

He ran thus till he came at a place somewhat ascending, and upon that place stood a cross, and a little below, in the bottom, a sepulchre. So I saw in my dream, that just as Christian came up with the cross, his burden loosed from off his shoulders, and fell from off his back, and began to tumble, and so continued to do, till it came to the mouth of the sepulchre, where it fell in, and I saw it no more.

—Pilgrim's Progress

She was back and sitting on the edge of the chair as the flannel piece burden fell off Christian's back and rolled down the hill and suddenly vanished into the stacks of other pieces on the table. With bright eyes and wide-open mouth, she gasped as the answer sank into her brain.

She needed to share this news with her twin sister. "The answer is the cross! I heard the evangelist say that in the meeting last night. He said to lay your burden down at the foot of the cross. We can go to the foot of the cross and get rid of the dark cloud of sin!"

The small eight-year-old glowed with her new understanding. And her twin companion began to think about how they could accomplish getting to the foot of the cross.

The twin who had been secretly listening to the Story Lady said, "Didn't she tell us angels would be our guide? Didn't angels guide Christian? When people go down to the front of the tabernacle and cry and get up happy, does that mean it is the foot of the cross? Will angels help me there so the dark cloud will leave?"

They began talking to each other at the same time but somehow came up with a plan. The small Pilgrim would walk down the long aisle in the tabernacle—just like Christian had walked down the long path between the walls. She would go to the altar and find an angel to help her. The other twin who carried the burden would explain the problem to the angel and the angel would know how to make the burden fall off.

The plan was set. They waited for the evening meeting and as the service came to a close, the little Pilgrim waited patiently for the evangelist to stop talking. When he told people to come to the foot of the cross, she was off! It was a very long aisle, but she was very brave. She got to the front and knelt at the altar. Suddenly, an angel kneeled across from her and reached out to hold her hands.

"Dr. Sue, why are you here?" The adult me was suddenly confused. I was listening and following the children during EMDR therapy, so of course she was there; but she didn't belong in the memory! Here she was at the altar holding my hands. This made no sense, but I kept on.

The small child began talking to the angel, "I came to get rid of my burden of sin. It is my dark cloud and I came for it to fall off here at the foot of the cross."

She prayed and asked for forgiveness, then got up and walked away—with the dark cloud still hovering over her.

My eyes opened. I stared at Dr. Sue. We both tried to understand what had just happened.

My thoughts slowly formed into words, "She thought the dark cloud was sin...."

By this time, we had found and healed the memory of the dark cloud, but of course these children couldn't know what it was. They thought it was sin. How tragic.

Dr. Sue was thinking too. "The cloud wasn't sin. The dark cloud was the emotions and pain from the abuse."

"Yes. The flannelgraph piece of Christian's burden looked just like the dark cloud hovering over me. I thought it was sin and by going to the altar it would be like the foot of the cross, and it would fall off. But it didn't."

My mind reeled. What do the lessons we teach children about sin, say to those children who have suffered abuse? They already feel it was probably their fault, and then when they seek help, we call the turmoil inside them sin.

At the very end of the memory, there was a sense of the child going back to the altar a second time—in fact, every year at camp, at every age, I would go to the altar to try to rid myself of the dark cloud. It never went away until the three year old was healed. My entire life, this little eight year old never gave up searching for the answer to the dark cloud hovering over her.

Abruptly, the confusion about Dr. Sue's presence in my memory returned.

"Did you hear me? You were there in the memory. Or at least I thought you were. A woman came to help the eight year old who went down to the altar. She looked like you. She looked exactly like you. She took my hands in hers, just exactly like you do at the end of therapy. I trusted you immediately that first session and have never understood it because I never trusted anyone. The little eight-year-old Pilgrim inside of me thought she had found her angel again."

With this epiphany, all the small parts of me smiled at Dr. Sue and she, somewhat surprised, smiled back at them.

How sad to know these small twins had tried so hard and failed. Their willingness to keep looking for the answers amazed me. Slowly, I began to recognize the dark cloud as the shame from the abuse and surrounding circumstances. Shame was the cloud that followed me every day. For two years, the layers of shame kept surfacing until one day, almost at the very end of therapy, we found one of these twins had been hiding most of the shame with her in the Basement of Shame. I was going to need to spend some time in that basement in order to fully understand my story, but for now these twins seemed to have told all they wanted to tell.

14
Upper Elementary Years

Two sets of twins lived my life from fourth to sixth grade. I came to know them as Nine and The 5th Grader; but it took some time before I realized they each had a twin. Both sets hid their twin sisters for most of therapy. Jeannie was maturing and the roles of the twins were becoming increasingly complicated. There was additional trauma, most of which the children chose not to share. The Nine Year Old Who Lives became a warrior, and her twin who hid because she lost her voice, was my little bookworm and writer.

By the time I turned ten, we had moved away from Albuquerque, leaving my support system behind. Now my soul contained an infant, a three year old, two sixes, two sevens, two eights and two nines. I was exactly the age my oldest brother had been when he was commissioned into caring for me, so it made sense that the ten-year-old fifth grader would become the Older Sibling to all the dissociated children frozen inside me. The stress on my system was overwhelming, and the Older Sibling's twin, the Comforter, was in charge of finding a way to soothe the system. What she did was pure genius.

As I pondered what to tell, I noticed Jeannie was back, looking over my shoulder.

"You know you could write a whole book about these two," she said.

She was right. "What do you think we should tell?"

She thought for a while and said, "Well, we need to tell about the wedding and about how Nine loved *The Wizard of Oz* and wanted to go to the Emerald City. Our oldest brother left for college the year I turned nine. Maybe that is why she had to be a warrior. She had to learn to take care of herself."

THE YEAR OF INDEPENDENCE

The gift the Eights gave to Nine was the result of a bribe. They begged and begged to join Brownies and had just gotten started when it came time to sell cookies. This was a problem, because the preacher's children couldn't sell at church, even though everyone else was. Also, the preacher's family was busy on Saturday and didn't have time to take a child around to sell cookies—but an eight-year-old could not go alone. It was a problem—one solved by a bribe.

"If you will agree not to go to Brownies anymore, I will buy you the bike you want." Jeannie agreed; and though her mother had broken many bribes before, this time her mother came through with the promised bike. No one wanted to help Jeannie learn to ride it; so she went to the side of the house to teach herself. Through sheer perseverance, and after many bruises, she learned to stay upright and moving.

This was the bike Nine inherited, and it was her ticket to independence. She was either on her bike or reading a book, but she also loved hopscotch and playing King of the Hill on the mounds of dirt next to the church. Nine was active but oddly failed PE. It was something about refusing to do wheel barrow relay races in a dress in front of the male PE teacher. She refused and sat beside the field but never told anyone why.

Nine didn't really like her teacher, but her favorite part of the school day was after lunch when the teacher read portions of a book aloud—possibly the only time Nine sat still. When recess came, she was out of the room like a shot to claim the best hopscotch with well-worn grooves in the dirt.

She received handle grips with streamers for her bike as a present. She proudly put them on only to have them come off in her hands and send her flying over the handlebars. Nine just got up. She was tough that way.

Nine often rode barefoot, because there was such a commotion if her shoes got scuffed. She scraped off the end of her big toe and couldn't get her Sunday shoes on. Her mother was very upset, because this made her miss church. She really did try to stay out of trouble, but that was mostly impossible for such a busy child.

This child enjoyed her independence and named her bike Bluebird. She thought maybe she could fly over the rainbow where troubles melt like lemon drops. It was not to be so.

OVER THE RAINBOW

Early in therapy, I had realized the song from *The Wizard of Oz* held significance. I was never sure why until the children began to surface.

Midway through the second year of therapy, while sitting in a Denver Starbucks, "Somewhere Over the Rainbow" began playing over the speakers. The room began to spin as I fought to stay grounded in my chair. What was up with this song? It had caused me to cry in yoga before therapy began. The Three Chairs had spent an entire evening playing it over and over as what appeared to be grief poured out of them. Now, here I was dissociating in Starbucks because of this song.

Making my way to the restroom, I tried to pull myself together. Regaining my composure, I moved into the nearby atrium to search for and listen to the song.

... Somewhere, over the rainbow, bluebirds fly.
Birds fly over the rainbow; why, oh why, can't I?

—E. Y. Harburg, lyricist

There it was ... bluebirds! My bike was named Bluebird because of this song! My child self was longing to fly over the rainbow, to wake up where the dark cloud was far behind her, where troubles would melt like lemon drops.

This nine-year-old warrior kept me walking every day. She was the one who shifted into every trauma from the age of nine and then got up and walked every "next day." She will never give up on this dream—just as she had never given up on leaving the cloud far behind her. Nine is my inner warrior.

Nine hid her twin sister who had been traumatized one day while reading a book. I found many places in my writing where Nine said she was not a twin. Yet, I couldn't seem to define the one who would step in and begin writing the most fanciful, delightful pieces. She spoke through my writing. The warrior closely guarded her so we would not see her.

One day this quiet twin got caught in an EMDR memory and couldn't get out of the room fast enough. She was terrified. Dr. Sue saw the fear and said something to the effect of, "We need to finish this before we leave."

What this frightened child heard was, "We need to leave."

Consumed by shame for staying too long, the child took off running. I saw her running down the hallway in my mind and began to gather my things to leave. Dr. Sue took my hands, placed them on my lap, and continued therapy. The child did not fight her.

We laughed about this later, because it was as if she pulled her back by the scruff of her neck. I am grateful she did. This was how we found my bookworm writer—but she had no voice. It would take some time to understand why not, and that will be included in the sequel to this book.

THE OLDER SIBLING

Traveling to Seattle, which by the way is known as The Emerald City, is always high on my list of favorite things to do. Spending time with family is the reason. My grandchildren and my daughter shared houses with us for most of ten years, and I miss them every day, but on this day, my grandchildren and I were together.

It was disconcerting to realize being left to care for my grandchildren irritated someone inside of me. How could this be? Thinking back over the years, this tendency was evident but had never been understood. Now it was out of control. I was an exceedingly irritated ten-year-old child. This was how the Older Sibling became visible. Being left with the children was a trigger. This very competent Older Sibling stepped in to take on the responsibility—but she was not happy in doing so.

I emailed Dr. Sue: "Another child has appeared!" We were not surprised. It was time to begin understanding her.

Up until my fifth-grade year, while living in Albuquerque, I had the loving support of my church family. Leaving this home was very difficult despite my love for California. Where we landed was isolated and lonely—and my mother hated it instantly. My parents' decision to move to this location, sight unseen, never really made sense. My brother had gone to spend the summer at my aunt and uncle's farm in Colorado and I was, for the most part, alone with my mother. The dirt roads and busy highway were not conducive to riding my bike, and there were no friends. It was a dramatic change.

There was one girl my age in the church, but her family left soon after our arrival. Susan and I have remained friends and spent time at each other's houses and even roomed together for a semester in college. I visited her the year the children surfaced. She related how her mother asked my mother how she liked it there. My mother answered, "What is there to like?"

Yes, it was a lonely summer with my mother who hated where we had moved.

My dad had some health issues that year and acted very different from the father I had always known. This was a dramatic change. A set of twins who could navigate the new landscape of my life was needed. One twin had the specific responsibility of caring for the younger children so the other could live. The children all held pain and triggers, so she was very busy. She needed to find ways to help them.

One day, at the corner market, she spotted a kitten meowing in a box. She had never had a pet, but she was sure this kitten would help the children. She marched home and almost demanded she be allowed to bring the kitten home. My parents, who must have seen it as a solution for my unhappiness, agreed. I named him Blue Boy. This kitten became one of a long line of cats adopted for the purpose of caring for myself.

THE FRIEND MAKER GOES TO SCHOOL

Until this fifth-grade year, making friends had always been a non issue. My friends had been in the nursery with me, and we grew up together. We chased lizards and played King of the Hill while the adults talked endlessly after church. My neighborhood overflowed with children, and I was well liked at school. But now, in my loneliness, I needed friends. And I didn't just want a friend; I wanted to be liked by everyone. To this end, the ten-year-old version of the One Who Lives was extremely successful. That year I learned to make friends—it was an important skill for the remainder of my life.

My memories of this year are filled with a sense of belonging to a group of friends. We played hard at recess—four-square, climbing on the monkey bars, and on a large, painted map of the United States. I enjoyed climbing on farm equipment at a friend's farm and running through bamboo pathways around a reservoir. When alone, my favorite activity was to run with the wind—which constantly blows on the high desert. I would go to the end of the field and wait for a gust. Running with the wind and leaping over sagebrush felt distinctly like flying.

My friendship skills went awry only once. A girl in my class, who had probably suffered many wrongs in her young life, wanted to be part of our group. To do this, she created fanciful stories about a boyfriend who bought her dresses. We knew it wasn't true but played along to see how many stories she would create. It was one of two "mean girl" episodes in my generally kind life. When she realized what we were doing, she told the teacher. I loved my teacher. Her disappointment in me was devastating.

My co-conspirator and I were sitting on a bench on the playground. Mrs. Schultz stood in front of us with the sun behind her, looking at us with sad, brown eyes. Two of her girls had been so thoughtless and mean to another child. The Ten Year Old Who Lives had caused the problem, but all the children were in distress. When the teacher moved slightly, the sun flashed into my eyes. At that moment the realization of what I had done struck me.

Then, as I began floating in a way I'd never before experienced, my body flooded with a sensation of complete relaxation. A twin, the Comforter, had arrived on the scene.

This new floating experience was extremely effective in helping to calm everyone; the Comforter thought it could be repeated. She practiced it by going back to that moment again and again. It was some type of very effective dissociation that I eventually began to understand as a protective coping mechanism. It left me relaxed but completely ungrounded. Repeating the experience was dependent on a connection with a caring authority-type figure, which would get complicated, as I grew older. It was a survival-based, dissociative self-care skill fraught with complications, but it probably saved my life and prevented many stress-related health problems. My dependency on this child's method of self care created layers of shame. These were very difficult to release until I understood the dissociative strategy as a skill developed by a very clever ten-year-old child!

The Older Sibling made friends with peers, but the Comforter gravitated toward adults. If she trusted an adult it was a great honor! She was an expert at building a self-care village. During times of stress, she always surfaced to take care of me. She worked hard during the two years of therapy to keep me from collapsing. Other self-care strategies seemed less effective to her. Helping her not feel responsible for me all the time was challenging. The number of ways this twin cared for me just kept surfacing. She had even learned to drive, but that is a story for the children's book.

Once again, these twins worked so closely it was some time before they were distinguishable. The system of one who lives and one who holds the pain was adapted to the friend maker who lives and the one who cares for and comforts children. It was the same theme with different roles.

How Teachers Cared

Before my fifth grade year was over, we had moved again. It was inevitable—remember, my mother hated it there. Our new location was an improvement, but leaving my friends behind was sad. A house in a suburb with lots of children proved even better, though, and I could ride my bike again.

But my mother needed to finish her teaching contract. So she rented a small apartment in town where she taught and my brother attended high school. For the rest of the year, I would have to leave the country school I had been attending, and then go to yet *another* school the following year.

Then my teacher stepped in. She lived in town and offered to pick me up every day on her way to the country school. For probably two months she listened to my chatter all the way to school and back home again. I was in heaven! I am sure she missed the time to get her head together on the way to school and her quiet ride on the way back home. What a marvelous gift she gave me. We kept in touch for many years but eventually lost contact during one of my later moves.

For more than thirty years I trained future teachers, and this story was embedded in my first lecture. Now that I better understand the challenges I was living with during those elementary years, I appreciate even more the gift of friendship this teacher gave me.

I was that kid who always wanted and needed to have the teacher's attention. While delightful and bright, my need for attention must have been taxing. She filled me up to overflowing and sent me off to the next school believing teachers would take care of me and help me survive.

The next year also proved fortunate. In a new school up the hill from our suburban neighborhood, Miss Knox became my sixth grade teacher. My mother taught in the same school, and I often waited to ride home with her—but spent my time with my teacher. Once again, I was that child, but this teacher was also willing to give me attention.

My neighborhood and the church were a village for me again. We rode bikes and spent hours playing with Barbie dolls—the best new doll in America. I became an expert double-Dutch jump rope twirler and enjoyed going to the eucalyptus grove and climbing up to sit in the trees and drown in the leaves' aroma.

It could have been a perfect two years—and in almost every way it was. If only I had not been conditioned to dissociate when in danger. This would prove to be tragic.

Reinterpreting a Wedding

Looking back over the entire landscape of my childhood, it is apparent I was determined to live despite the trauma, which seemed to follow me. In order to do this, it was often necessary to tell a different story—or to reinterpret dissociative episodes in ways that weren't exactly correct but made sense. My oldest brother's wedding was one of those.

Lee left for college at the beginning of my fourth-grade year. I grieved his absence. Soon he was telling us he had found the woman of his dreams. She wrote me letters about being a sister; and my child self was always hoping someone would come along to pay attention to me, so I was hopeful. The only problem was, she and my brother were so in love, they could only see each other.

Upon moving to California, our home was close enough for my brother and his fiancée to come visit. Lee was instantly in the awkward place of having two siblings and a fiancée all wanting his attention. My other brother and I lost the contest. There was no way to compete with true love. There was really no way for anyone to win in this situation fraught with jealousy for time and attention.

When wedding plans were announced for the spring, it was devastating—the final blow. I was losing my brother to her. We traveled some distance to the wedding and my loss was felt during every mile. Arriving at the church, I wandered around feeling sad and alone. The ending to this story—the one I always told—was that I had refused to sit with my family during the ceremony and, instead, watched the wedding from a hiding spot in the balcony.

This story began to crumble in a conversation with my cousin who knew nothing of my absence.

She said, "But I was in the wedding, so it could have happened, I just don't remember."

Surely my mother would have made a scene upon my return to the family. And it was unlikely someone would not have been looking for me.

The memory of the wedding surfaced during EMDR therapy, and I saw myself walking in and sitting with my family. Wait! Try as I might to replay the memory my way, the memory would not go there. The true memory always placed me in the row with my parents. No one was looking for me, because I wasn't missing. Yet, the wedding did seem to be viewed from the balcony....

"Dr. Sue, I dissociated at the wedding! I was floating on the ceiling. My story of the balcony was a way to explain the dissociation. It must have been so confusing to me."

Actually there was a lot that was confusing. Children with dissociative disorders are hard to understand, and they cannot understand themselves. Their dissociative strategies protect them from the overwhelming pain but also put them in danger and cause them to be misunderstood.

HEALING THE COMFORTER

The last child to heal was the Comforter. It made sense. She needed to take care of me until I could care for myself. Comforting was her role, but she also had memories to heal. Healing the Comforter was the final piece of the puzzle; but her story fits here because she was ten. Although the memory she needed to heal took place before the moving, before going to a new school, and before the wedding, she took the very longest to surface and heal.

As told earlier, the year I turned ten my family moved to California. There were many layers involved in this. Early in therapy, I realized it was a pivotal time period because I lost my support systems—school, teachers, church, friends, adults in the church, and my beloved campgrounds. I even had to leave my chair behind.

The move was troubling in many ways, and somewhere in this timeline additional abuse occurred. I made a promise to my father to never talk about it. It was the gulf between us I could never put my finger on. The promise, along with the abuse, was repressed but always held inside of me—until after we thought we had finished our work in therapy.

I was finalizing the book. Dr. Sue and I were working through some sections. Therapy had ended, but one day I knew something was wrong. Much to my dismay, I understood something was surfacing. I called to leave a message and was surprised when she answered on her busy day.

"I need to talk!" I blurted out.

Well, that was awkward.

Collecting myself, I tried to explain and we made an appointment for the next day. After hanging up, I realized I had shifted. Overcome with discouragement, I faced the reality that someone was not fully healed. I started looking for clues.

Scott and I had been discussing the prospect of moving. The end of Scott's employment was looming closer, and we were exploring our options. Did this very real possibility of moving trigger a shift? The adult me was not upset we might move closer to family; but if a child were not healed, what would she feel?

"It is Ten," I informed Dr. Sue.

This made sense to both of us. I explained that I had awakened in a deeply depressive state. Two days before, I had a dream that seemed like it might be connected to her. It also seemed to have something to do with the fact I was beginning to share my story in speaking venues. With every effort toward telling my story, waves of panic set in.

What exploded out of me during EMDR was possibly the most emotional flood yet. Something happened to me and I didn't understand that I had dissociated. My dad asked me to promise that I would never tell what had happened. I never did. I never will. I will keep the promise.

What I understand now is I generalized the promise to every abuse which occurred after that day. The following section is filled with tragic stories in which no one was ever held accountable because my subconscious memory of a promise kept me silent. This was not what my father intended. I understand why he made me promise, but he would be heartbroken to know it kept me silent in situations where I should have spoken.

Between my dissociative tendencies, my ability to repress almost instantly, and my promise never to tell, I could not stop the swiftly moving train of abuse that had begun when I was three and just kept picking up speed.

REINTERPRETING A CHILDHOOD

During my childhood there were times when my family would just shrug and say something like, "Well, OK, Janyne. If you say so." My cover stories never made sense, not even to myself, but they were necessary for survival. I do wonder how often I was dissociating and unclear about what I thought was truth.

There is a concern this story of my life will only be viewed as another rendition of my fanciful childhood tales....

Jeannie, who had been allowing me to tell the stories, watched me closely as this concern was typed.

I looked at her. "You have always been afraid you would not be believed if we told the story. You were never believed as a child, and I didn't believe you either. My adult self could not accept the awful things that happened. We know the truth now. We may not remember everything exactly right, but we corrected many of our stories during EMDR therapy. All of it finally makes sense. No matter what happens, I believe you."

She seemed satisfied. She also appeared to be a whole child despite being made up of such a mixture of child parts. She was a healed, healthy child, and she was getting restless.

"Jeannie, we are finished telling the children's stories. Maybe there will be more to tell later; but for now, the story ends. It's time for you to go play."

Skipping away, she left the stuffed puppies and large doll behind. She was holding tight to the hand of the White Rabbit who led her to where her bike was waiting. Then, in the white fluffy clouds above me, I saw her ride toward a rainbow with a string of bluebirds behind her.

The Emerald City was glowing in front of her. I hoped she would find a land where she could play hopscotch to her heart's content while her troubles melted away like lemon drops way above the chimney tops.

She turned and waved to me before she vanished out of sight. She would always live inside my heart. Everything I am is because this child found a way to live.

15
Middle School Years

Early in therapy, it became evident the Three Chairs had not always existed. While creating a timeline of my life, I realized, for the most part, I had always lived at two levels. These two levels appeared to be exactly like Janyne and Jane. The controlling Non Janyne did not appear until much later. My structures during the teen years were like the children's system of twins—the one who lived (Janyne) and the one who held the pain (Jane). The world saw Janyne; but in photographs, Jane's dark pain is visible in my eyes. It was probably perceived as teenage angst and moodiness.

The same pattern continued during my young adult years, but with a significant change in my beliefs about myself. The pain I lived above as a teenager settled into my being. The implied messages became a spoken message and changed me in damaging ways.

There were two versions of Janyne and Jane during my teens and young adults. The pain within the frozen children prevented integration, but my structures usually allowed me to appear to live as one person. This meant living as Janyne, but during times of duress, Jane would appear.

It is difficult to explain the degree to which dissociation continued to affect my life. It might have been possible to protect myself during these middle-school years, but I had been conditioned for mental and emotional escape instead. I had been shushed and not believed so often that my only choice was to float up to the ceiling, avoid the pain, and get up and walk away as if nothing happened. This made me a perfect target.

THE CARNIVAL IS COMING TO TOWN!

Once he had taken hold, he did not let go.
It was not a handshake, it was a possession.

—Lisa Klyepas

Our excitement could barely be contained. My friends and I were twelve, and the carnival was coming to town. It wasn't just coming to town; it was going to be set up in the field next to our subdivision. Somehow, being able to see the bright lights and hear the music from our houses made it all the more exciting. We discussed the rides we would take … before I became the ride.

A partial memory of what happened always remained. In my memory, I was at a friend's house, waiting for her to come home from an errand, when teenage boys called to me from one of the bedrooms. I did remember being playfully jostled around the room before being pushed onto a bed and touched. I also remembered writing a friend and telling her about being touched—and how her mother said she couldn't communicate with me anymore. My inexplicable behavior during my seventh-grade year was seemingly unconnected. This was all true, as far as it went, but much had also been repressed.

"Hello, you must be Rich's sister." He was older, and he seemed nice. My awkward preteen self felt honored by his attention. He was one of three in the room. I accepted his handshake.

There it was. For weeks, this memory had been trying to surface. What had always been a distaste for shaking hands had recently morphed into a pathological fear, which finally made me stomp my feet and say, "No!" to a hapless church greeter. The trauma had been trying to escape through almost violent shaking; but I could never make the connection between shaking hands and any of my trauma memories—until I remembered this hand being stretched out to me in a seeming act of friendship.

In an earlier session, Dr. Sue had tried to help me find a connection.

"What do you feel when a man is going to shake your hand?"

My outburst was a surprise to both of us, but her eyes never wavered when my answer came out completely unfiltered and graphic. It was shocking. I didn't know who had said it, but if this was how I felt, it was no wonder I was struggling. Still, the memory did not surface.

My subconscious didn't give up the memory easily. First, I had to realize my cover story of being touched and running out of the room wasn't true. All of my stories of "brave me" were cover stories used to bury the truth about how I always dissociated and "froze" during rapes. In all the memories, everything up to the point when the rape began was remembered, but the subsequent trauma was repressed. Then it was necessary to realize there was not just one teenage boy, nor two, but three.

It took several EMDR sessions before my body completely released the trauma.

My hand offered in friendship was grabbed, and I was shoved around the room among the three, finally falling onto the bed. Until the bed was beneath me, it all just appeared to be playful teenage jostling. Then I felt the touch and floated to the ceiling and watched the ensuing horror through the fog.

"She doesn't even fight. She just lies there. Your turn. She's a great ride!"

The trauma was inside me. My soul was dying. The carnival was coming to town, and now I realized I was the ride the boys wanted to take.

By morning the memory was gone. Apparently, I got up the next day as if it had not happened but missed the carnival because of the measles. That was OK. I never really liked carnival rides anyway.

Inexplicable Behavior

The summer came and went and it was almost time to head to middle school. Before school began, I came down with pneumonia and simultaneously company arrived and took over my bedroom. Miserable and coughing, the couch was no comfort. No one was noticing this poor child on the couch coughing up her lungs, so I took my own temperature: 102°. My mother shook it down and said it was not reading correctly.

When the company left, I proclaimed imminent death, and was finally taken to a doctor. The doctor listened to me hacking and walked out, leaving a cigarette smoking in the ashtray. Fed up with no one taking care of me, and knowing it was possible my mother would have a meltdown over the cigarette smoke, I doused it in water. The doctor looked mildly irritated when he returned and tried to smoke his limp, wet cigarette. He looked at me as I coughed and glared at him.

This memory sums up my attitude during my seventh-grade year. If no one else was going to take care of me; I would have to do it myself. The child who left the secure confines of the neighborhood elementary school and the one who arrived in middle school were two different girls. Something had happened to change my behavior to a belligerent, unhappy child.

I was an angry seventh grader who desperately wanted someone to pay attention to me. Alas, my mother was in the midst of a mental breakdown over a church situation gone wrong. All eyes were on her.

One teacher might have sensed my distress. Her name was Mrs. Knuckles and she was not pleased with my constant disruption in her class. One day she stopped and sat across from me. She said, "Janyne, what is wrong? Your records do not indicate any behavior problems in the past. This isn't really like you, is it? Did something happen? Can you talk to me?"

No, it wasn't possible to talk to her, but we did come to an agreement. She would just smile at me at the beginning of class to let me know she believed my behavior would be acceptable. This was all I wanted or needed. I simply needed someone to see me and care.

She also said it might help me to keep a journal. She was a language arts teacher and knew of my love for reading and ability to write. The journal written during that year was carried with me always, but I could never bring myself to read it. It might have contained clues. But one day shortly before I began therapy, the dark cloud consumed me and I destroyed the journal in an attempt to escape from the darkness.

Maybe this teacher knew. She seemed to see the sadness behind my crooked-tooth smile. Once again a teacher stepped in and cared. She looked beyond my behavior and saw *me*. She stopped trying to control behavior and found a way to meet my unspoken needs.

Moving Again but Finding Family

We moved again before my seventh-grade year was over, and I had to commute an hour for school every day. Because of our many moves, my family spent copious amounts of time on southern California freeways as we travelled back for my mother to complete her contracts. I remember occupying myself by sending parts of me to ride on the tops of other cars. We would have races to our destination. This always seemed an odd thing for a twelve year old to do, but now it makes sense.

By the time the school year ended, my thirteenth birthday had come and gone. After a tolerable summer, during which a week was spent with a family at a beach cottage resulting in a serious sunburn, I was ready to start a new school year in yet another school. It appeared the angry seventh grader had been left behind. Though never able to completely stay out of trouble (due more to mischief than attitude), I felt less need to bring attention to myself.

On the first day of school, while moving from class to class and sitting in alphabetical order, Jenkins and Johnson appeared to have the exact same schedule. By the end of the day, we laughed, shrugged, and decided we should be friends. The friendship has stood the test of time.

Christina (whom I still call Christy) lived between my house and the school. My house was always empty until late afternoon, so it made sense to spend an hour or so at her house on my way home.

Walking in the door of my friend's house was like entering a completely different world. There was a carp pond in the back yard with a huge iguana in a nearby cage. Every form of fauna grew in both the front and back yards. The house was filled with words and writing. When I stayed for dinner, we all played Hink Pink (a clue results in one-syllable rhyming words, such as: large feline=fat cat). I was introduced to Star Trek and seriously considered the possibility of aliens and flying saucers. The house was decorated with paintings and whimsical cutout gourds with stairways and rooms for very small imaginary creatures. The cat's name was Toccata. Classical music filled the air. There was a darkroom in the garage, and I fell in love with photographs. Much of my creativity can be found in my memories of this house where imagination was as necessary as food.

Most importantly, there was a mother who waited for children to arrive home. She soon learned I loved strawberry milk and kept it in the cupboard for me.

"We were almost out of the strawberry milk powder, Janyne. I bought a new can, but there is still some left in the old one."

No matter where my family moved during the next ten years, this house remained my home. To this day, it is the only street address I can recall.

Then This Happened

Buried in this wonderful year was one tragic day. The story I have always told is this: I was babysitting a baby after school. The parents' work schedule overlapped, and there was a two-hour window when they needed someone to watch the baby. Wonderful! Spending money! Usually the baby just napped. One day the father got home early and came and sat down on the couch beside me—and got "handsy." I walked outside to stand by the car until he came out and drove me home.

Dr. Sue and I were talking about this memory when she asked where the baby was when he took me home. It was a simple question; but my world began to spin. My memory didn't make sense. Where was the baby? I wouldn't have just left the baby.

Then I remembered freeing myself from a groping hand and saying, "I need to check on the baby."

"I am standing over the crib. I feel breathing on my neck. 'If you come quietly with me and do what I say, I will take you home. If you fight or scream, you will scare the baby. You don't want to scare the baby do you?'

"The baby is sleeping—little butt in the air with legs tucked under. I am gazing at the few tufts of curls and the sweet little place on the neck, which always makes me smile. No, I cannot frighten a baby.

"I am in the hallway. I try to pull away. 'Shhhh.' He has hold of my arm and is pulling me to the back of the house. I am floating. I think he is someone else who told me 'Shhhh.' I know what he is going to do. I am little. I can't fight, because I am little."

Sinking back on the couch, I tried to make sense of it.

"I said someone else, didn't I? When he told me to shush, it was a trigger and I think I was suddenly six and he was someone else. I was as tall as I am now, but I felt little. I didn't think I could fight. I just floated and let him do that to me. I couldn't defend myself. First it was not scaring the baby, and then it was because I shifted and floated."

The pile of tissues was growing next to me on the couch as I continued to explain the ending of the true memory I had seen.

"Yes, I did eventually go out and stand by the car and wait for him to come out and drive me home—this time with the baby. I told him it would be my last day as their babysitter. He told me no one would believe me. We both knew it was true."

When I arrived home, Brussels sprouts where sitting on my dinner plate. I asked to go eat in my room and went out the back door and fed them to the ducks. This was a cover story to explain how I had always disliked Brussels sprouts. It wasn't true before that day. My family laughs at my complete abhorrence of a vegetable. It was kind of odd—I couldn't even bring myself to look at them.

My mother was angry when I told her I would not be baby-sitting anymore.

"These people are depending on you. You can't stop baby-sitting without giving them notice. What will they do? They have just started attending the church, and they will probably leave."

Once again, I was difficult. But it was only one bad day in an otherwise good year. It was hardly a bump in my happy-life story. I fed the Brussels sprouts to the ducks, made up a "brave me" cover story, repressed the memory, accepted being called difficult, and moved on. Despite the trauma, the overall stability of that year helped me create a teenage "me" who would excel at living. And we would soon move again.

16
Teenage Years

During my high school years we moved twice. I attended two high schools. My brother had it worse. He attended four. Our family, during my early childhood, had lived in one town for ten years. But after that we could not find stability. This paralleled my mother's mental health. She couldn't find balance either; but finally, after the fifth move she settled in. My parents tried to move again before my senior year. When I told them they would be going without me, they believed me and stayed.

It is important to note I did not come even close to reaping what my trauma should have caused—internally, yes, but not externally. There were three reasons for this. One was my strong core and belief in myself. The second was my dissociative structures, which enabled me to compartmentalize. Third was my outwardly normal life, which included my dad's support and that of many teachers and camp counselors.

Yes, my relationship with my mother was fraught with landmines, and I often felt invisible, but my home life was not chaotic. Unfortunately, this is not the case with most abused children. In many ways I consider myself fortunate.

One positive aspect of living with a dissociative disorder was the ability to live as a completely normal teenager apart from the inner turmoil. This doesn't mean that the inner turmoil did not exist; it just didn't register consciously with 'Janyne'—the one who lived. Yet, Jane (the one who held the pain), was always there, ready to surface. She was not just a moody teen side of me; she was a distinct personality.

To my readers this chapter may feel disjointed, disconnected, and often contradictory. Exactly. At any given moment, I was one of two different teenagers. The two teen parts of me saw the world very differently. Teen Jane was depressed, often angry, and at one point believed she was possessed by demons. Teen Janyne, on the other hand was successful in school, enjoyed friends, was involved at church, did all the things that teens love to do . . . and lived peaceably with my mother despite the lack of emotional relationship.

LIVING WITH MOTHER

It is necessary for teenagers to simply live life. My life involved my mother. My recollections of home during my high school years feel like a series of memory flashes. I was always just a bit outside of my life.

My needs were not on my mother's list very often, and my role was to be "useful." One day while walking through the kitchen, she said, "Janyne will you reach the bowl? I will be sad when you go to college because I will have to get the step stool out to reach things in the cupboard."

Yes, I was useful.

My goal was figuring out how to live my life around my mother. My love for clothes meant I needed to go shopping with her. This was a problem, because she was so unpredictable. It is hard to explain the anxiety; we never knew what she would say or do. She was abrupt and demanding, and it seemed necessary to follow behind her and talk winsomely to the sales people she had just insulted. It was a form of protecting our family honor. One way to do this was to tell the sales people some interesting tale about what had brought me to the store. This odd and awkward habit followed me my entire life.

One day I was sick and my mother told me to stay in my room. She brought me food, opened the door, slid the food in on the floor, and closed the door. I felt like a prisoner. Another time, my back went out while opening the bathroom door and I managed to get back to the bed where my body felt paralyzed. Yelling for help wasn't effective since my parents, who were in the kitchen talking, just kept yelling back, "If you need something, you will have to come here." *Ummmm, I can't?*

Eating out was an all-time favorite and my parents would often tell me they were leaving to go to a restaurant, and they said if I was ready in five minutes, I could go with them. For food, speed records were often set. But sometimes the swiftly-moving train left without me. Coming home to an empty house, I was never sure where they were or when they would return. Leaving a note was a foreign concept.

Then there was the day of the Wastebasket War. When we moved into the house, a wastebasket had been placed in my room. It wasn't my favorite, but it was functional. One day, my mother walked in, picked it up and said, "I need this."

There was no explanation for my rage. Nothing was ever mine, and what she gave, she took back. She never asked permission to enter my room. Lunging from my bed, we were suddenly both on the floor wrestling over a wastebasket. I won.

My mother liked to get the mail, which was dropped through a slot in the door. I would hear it drop and race for it, probably just to frustrate her. I felt it was necessary to win in small ways. On one particularly warm day, the front door was open, so the mail carrier just opened the screen and dropped the envelopes on the floor.

I heard the screen door slam shut and jumped into action.

My mother saw me coming and ran fast, bending over to get the mail while still in motion. The next thing I saw was her butt in the air, her heels flying off, and her body pushing the screen open as she landed on the porch. I fell to the floor laughing. She was not appreciative.

The kitchen was off limits when my mother cooked. Clean up was my responsibility. This arrangement worked for me, but I found it irritating she never tried to be tidy. (She never taught me to cook, but she did give me a cookbook for my wedding.)

My mother did teach me how to mend my clothes. I am good at mending, but needle threading is deadly. My eyes don't focus well, and she would watch me with impatience. Tying a knot in the thread had to be accomplished with perfection. With all our moves, I never had a home economics classes. Despite this, a friend taught me to sew and, ignoring the anxiety, my limited sewing lessons enabled me to make a couple dresses.

My household job was dusting, which required great attention to detail—with Q-tips. The tasks I was given were exacting, but once accomplished I had great freedom in planning my days. It was a strange kind of coexistence. I tried to be in my room or gone as much as possible. I avoided conversations because, inevitably, something I said would be turned against me. She had little trust for me.

Outwardly, everything needed to look perfect. Our house was always immaculate, but if you opened a drawer, it exploded with randomness. I, on the other hand, liked very neatly arranged drawers and was not opposed to leaving something out until it found a logical home. While I was at school, my mother would often come into my room, open the top drawers, and sweep everything off the dresser into my tidy organization.

My cats were my survival and comfort, and my mother

tolerated them. One cat had a litter of kittens under her bed. I found them there after a long search. They would have been fine there for a while, but it was not possible to leave them! I got a box and put them all in the garage, but the mother cat dragged all the kittens up the trellis to the roof. *What?* Keeping my cats from being an irritation to my mother gave me a constant challenge!

These events are rather innocuous and common in families, but my mother's intrusions and inconsiderate actions, without any form of true mothering, triggered the tension and rage inside my abused soul in ways which were difficult to understand. My level of anger always caused guilt. Even as a teenager, I felt my reactions were incongruent with my life, which was not a horrible life. Every morning my dad opened my bedroom door and called me "genius." A great way to start a day. No, my rage never made sense to me.

Hiding Jane

My friends who knew me in high school would describe me as the part I call "teen Janyne." They would have seldom seen "teen Jane." They may have caught glimpses of her, but they saw no obvious signs of abuse or trauma.

The summer after my junior year in high school, I was selected to represent my church district at a national teen convention. This was an honor. Qualifying required scripture memorization (not ever a strong skill), providing evidence of leadership and character, and a dreaded interview. It was a big deal.

The event took place in Estes Park, Colorado. Teens came from across the country. Part of our daily routine was to complete a devotional/self reflection. One of the prompts asked us to draw a picture of what we looked like inside. During therapy, this was one of the "clues" found in the boxes I had kept. My picture looked like a ball of twine created by a very young child. Who the world saw on the outside was certainly not who I understood myself to be on the inside.

Yet, the day I walked into therapy, my memories of my teen years are almost all positive. I did everything a healthy teenager should do: enjoying time with friends, swimming, going to the beach, Disneyland, camp, school activities, etc. Academics were not challenging, and my SAT scores earned me a California State Scholarship which paid 100% of my college tuition. I was a mischievous leader who was always looking for playful adventures with my posse of friends.

Living this life as a "normal" teenager, while so completely fractured, is astounding. While working with teens, we should never underestimate the power of the human spirit to rise above the pain—nor the amount of pain which can be concealed.

I did drop clues, though. While living the life of a "normal" teenager, there were occasional fleeting glimpses of Jane. It was necessary to find adults who would take an interest in me and help her. Teachers and camp counselors were my "go-to" options, and fortunately they did not betray my trust during my teen years. I learned to be the person others liked to be with and accepted their care while hiding the desperate neediness of Jane. This worked very well until tenth grade.

How Many Showers?

One day teen Jane showed up in therapy. During that particular session, she began to describe what her life had been like.

"I was always living above something. My tenth grade year was awful. We had moved again, and I could not make friends. I found a description of how I felt in a journal. It was tragic. I got shingles that year."

"Shingles? How old were you?"

"Fifteen? I was wearing orthodontic headgear at night and the shingles broke out under it. My hair covered it up until a teacher noticed the rash and sores. She sent me to the nurse. It was very painful, and I kept falling asleep; so they let me go to the nurse's office and sleep if tired. I went there often. It was an escape."

"What were you escaping?"

"Life? I didn't have friends at school. One girl ate lunch with me and suddenly she said, 'I don't know why we eat together, we don't have anything in common.' After that I ate alone. Mostly it was easier not to eat. I thought I was fat, anyway."

"Were you?"

"No, I would binge eat sometimes, but most of the time I was very thin.... Probably the worst time mentally was when I took all the showers."

"You took showers." Clearly, I had said something important.

"We were having youth group at church. A retired woman pastor was leading it, and she was having each of us give our testimony. My turn was coming—never a good thing. Suddenly I panicked, jumped up, ran from the church, and drove home and started taking showers—getting out and then getting back in."

"How many showers did you take?"

"Maybe ten? It felt like I couldn't get clean. I got in bed and started shaking. When my parents got home from church, they found me shaking under piles of blankets. My mother gave me one of her 'nerve pills.'"

I had always remembered this event, but I had detached myself from the emotions of it until now.

This session occurred early in therapy—before any rape memory surfaced. We did not find the meaning of the showers that day. We certainly could not connect "my turn is coming" to any memory at this point. From this day on, teen Jane was the one who came to therapy. She had finally been seen.

THE STORY KEPT GOING

I told Dr. Sue, "My obvious distress was a wake-up call to my parents, and I became more assertive in taking care of myself. It was impossible to handle the stress of going to school five days a week, so they allowed me to choose one day to stay home. They would have moved me to another school the following year if I had not made friends with the twins, Martha and Margaret, who were a year behind me. My junior and senior years were very different because of this friendship."

In hindsight, the day of the showers was a wake-up call for me, also. I realized there was something inside of me that had the potential to destroy me. It was possible to live above it, but Jane's pain was always a part of my life. She was always there with me. Sometimes she would step forward to talk to counselors at camp. They must have wondered why such a happy teenager would suddenly change into someone who appeared to be completely depressed. It didn't really make sense to me, either—and the voices in my head were always confusing.

THE BLUE ROOM

Another important teen memory surfaced at the end of the first phase of therapy. Believing I had gotten to a good place, we began to consider taking a break from therapy. Then, out of nowhere, the memory of the Blue Room arrived.

This memory surfaced during a quiet day in my office while pretending to work. This had become a common occurrence.

My outer life and the decisions needing to be made were monumentally stressful. My inner life was in turmoil and I couldn't comprehend why. The anxiety around waiting to hear about the job I had applied for, was palpable. A commitment to several outside obligations loomed over me and the bout of bronchial asthma from the mold was still affecting me. I could not seem to get well and was virtually immobilized ... and frustrated.

I also struggled with the desire to leave therapy. Clearly, even after all the progress we had made, my life-long battle with dependency was still part of the picture. I was still held captive. I could fake it, soldier through it, or tear myself from it; but any of those options belied the clear prompting God had given me to make an appointment with a particular therapist. Could God bring me healing? I had believed it then; but it was harder now. However, to admit failure was not part of my DNA.

Then I remembered my dream from the night before—a recurring dream that had visited me for many years. The dream had always felt significant, but this is the first time it had occurred during therapy. Grabbing paper, I quickly wrote a description of the dream to take to therapy that afternoon.

I am in a large blue room. There are empty chairs there and evidence this was once an active place, but it is now deserted. There seem to be voices outside. It feels like others should be there, but my voice echoes in the emptiness. It is very peaceful, yet unsettling. The room makes me anxious and fearful. There are clothes rods with hangers on them and a few odd pieces of clothing. They don't make much sense, but I may have worn them—

There the dream always ended.

The feelings in the dream settled into my soul—a sense of peace yet being unsettled at the same time. Everything was gone. It was like the emptiness in my life. This was new but vaguely familiar, and my purpose in it was not clear: alone in a big blue room with empty chairs and staring at the remnants of something which no longer existed.

Back in therapy, I did my best to explain the feelings and the blue room.

"Do we need to go to the blue room?"

"Yes—not sure why, but maybe so."

I am exploring the room. The tattered remnants hanging there are useless. I am going to sit in the chairs. None of them feel right. I feel like Goldilocks, because none of them fit. I don't want the chairs there. If I take them out, then I can fill the room with new things for my new life. I am carrying the chairs out. There is a ledge around the room so I have to lift them out. Oh! I am afraid! I am trying desperately to throw the chairs, but the harder I try, the stronger the terror. I have to leave the chairs behind and try to drag myself out. I am terrified by who I will find outside the room.

"Did you feel the terror grip me when I tried to climb out of the room?"

Dr. Sue affirmed the truth of this—it was intense.

"It was a familiar terror. The chairs had to be left behind to escape. Putting the chairs back was the only thing stopping the terror. Saying the room was empty wasn't really true. It was as if even acknowledging the chairs would bring the terror back."

The Winchester House

The session ended; but as the evening wore on, the memory of when this terror gripped me the first time began to surface. By the next session, the entire story was intact and ready to be told.

It was during high school, probably soon after I took all the showers. While staying with my brother in northern California, we decided to visit the Winchester House. The heir to the Winchester rifle fortune built this house after her husband and child died. She was convinced by a psychic she was being haunted by all those killed by the rifles her family had manufactured. The full story of the unexplainable mansion she built is fascinating, but in the center of the mansion was what they call the Blue Room. This is where she met nightly with the good spirits and they instructed her as to what the workers should build the next day.

The room was sunken and it was necessary to climb out— they had placed steps by one of the doors to help people out, but I was sixteen and determined to climb out on my own. But I felt something sucking me back into the room, as if spirits were grabbing at my legs to keep me in the room. It was terrifying. I pulled myself out, dazed. No one else appeared in any way affected. When I asked them, it seemed no one else experienced anything weird. The tour continued with me in a disoriented fog.

The terror was the same. In EMDR, in my version of the blue room, while trying to take the chairs out, there was a ledge all around the room and it was necessary to pull myself out with the chairs. It was the same feeling of terror.

The tour guide told the story about how Mrs. Winchester met with the spirits in the room and planned life. Maybe it connected at some subconscious level with my teenage self who could not understand all the voices in my head.

Mrs. Winchester had directed her life on command of the spirits. She convened with them every night. It makes sense how this story probably connected with my own subconscious reality. Maybe Janyne and Jane seemed like good and bad spirits, and the spirits in the room connected with them and tried to hold me there.

My life as a teenager was beginning to make sense—not that it made me feel comfortable to realize my teen self had been so emotionally unstable, but it did make sense. It was truly a stunning piece of processing. My web searches found pictures and descriptions. The connections with my recurring dream were clear.

Dr. Sue said, "I thought we might need to go back to the blue room."

I am in the room. I sense something. No one else seems to sense anything. The room is filled with blueness—as if covered in fog. The tour guide is talking. He is telling about the spirits who came to this room to talk to Mrs. Winchester. They told her what to do every day. She watched the house servants from this room. It feels very peaceful in this room. The guide is telling us we can leave. I am climbing out. No, I can't climb out! Something is grabbing my feet. I feel so heavy. I can't breathe. I keep trying, but something is pulling me down. Terror! I want to scream but I can't. I can't break free. Trying harder, the grip is loosening. I feel it loosening. It is inside of me. It is darkness. It is twined around the innermost part of me. It is loosening, more and more, and more. It stops. It isn't all gone, but I am out of the room.

I sank back into the couch in relief. "Oh. I thought I was

possessed by demons. I didn't understand it was my fractured soul. I thought they recognized demons in me and tried to keep me there. I don't know what was unwinding inside of me. I don't understand what it was. I will need to think about this more."

It took some time to get me to a place where it was safe to drive home.

BACK TO THE BLUE ROOM

Back in therapy, my words began as if I had boarded a slow-moving train that kept picking up speed. Soon the almost-incoherent words tumbled over each other.

"I don't know what it was. It was darkness intertwined around my core. It almost all left, but not all. It was like a huge tumor that twines itself into every part of a human body. I think it was the bad wiring in my head, the idea I was possessed by something I couldn't understand. Remember when I said I believed I held some kind of power over people and it caused them to fail or do bad things? Is this where the idea began? I can't live like this. I can't live my life continuing to fall off this cliff. We said I could be rewired."

"Yes, I thought we would probably need to go back to the Blue Room again today. Are you ready to go there?"

No words were necessary. She saw the desperate cry for help in my eyes.

"Tell me when you are in the room."

I'm in the room. It's peaceful. But the swirling is beginning at my feet. I hear the tour guide as if through a fog. The swirling has faces. They emerge, then vanish in the mist, and reappear in another place. I try to watch them. Their eyes look at me. They call to something inside of me.

They see something inside of me. They want me to stay here with them. They are creeping higher and higher on my legs.

The tour guide says we can leave. I lunge for the ledge to climb out, but they wrap themselves around my legs. 'Stay here with us. You belong here with us.' The terror grips me. I keep climbing. The weight, the heaviness. I can't breathe. I have to climb out. They force themselves into my soul. It is darkness there. I am almost out. Their grip is loosening. I feel them unwinding from my soul. Every part of me is releasing them and they are sliding back into the room. I am out.

I stared at Dr. Sue a long time, trying to process what had just happened. The memory of the swirling faces was there; but they no longer had control of me. Was my terror caused by my inner voices that could not be understood?

"I need to go back and tell my teenage self she was not possessed. They held no power over her! She thought spirits possessed her. This has been buried inside of me since sixteen!"

Sinking back into the memory and finding my teen self, the words began to burst out of me—loudly.

I have no spirits in me! You hold no power over me. You can't hold me any longer. I am free of you. I am free. I am not possessed. I was damaged. I needed help. You tried to capture me, but I have broken free. You will never hold power over me again. I am free.

Dr. Sue was watching me carefully as my eyes opened. "What are you feeling?"

"I'm not sure. I'm so sad for her, but she is free now. I think I am free, too, but I am going to have to try walking around to prove it."

Later, there would be another memory of the demons fighting over me. In an environment where everything is interpreted as a spiritual battle, my teen and young adult minds had nowhere else to turn for an explanation of the darkness I felt inside me. Many who suffer from dissociative disorders are re-traumatized by religious groups who believe they are demon possessed. This is not the case, but religious teaching without any understanding of dissociation caused me to think it was true.

The children tried to solve the problem. The teen thought it was demons, and demons fought over the young adult. This same darkness would be present on the cliff and it almost destroyed me. The Blue Room was the first time we located this darkness, but it would only be a few months before the six-year-old One Who Cries surfaced, believing she was dark inside.

By the time I returned for the next session, the most interesting realization had struck me.

"Sue, in every house we lived in during my adult years, I created a blue room."

"A blue room?"

"Yes. I always had a love-hate relationship with the color blue. It was as if it needed to be in my house, but at the same time, I didn't want it there. In different houses it was a kitchen, or a study, or a loft, or a bedroom; but it was always there."

Sometimes I fascinated both of us.

To put this in sequence, the first year of therapy was ending and it was time to take a break. I needed to rest before "the children" inside me showed up. Once the children arrived, I understood the faces I saw in the Blue Room were the children begging me to help them.

17
Young Adult Years

In this chapter, I am swiftly altered from the teenager who went to college feeling confident in her new world away from home. Yes, somehow, despite her repressed story, this teenager went to college with confidence and excitement. In one tragic day everything changed, though, and my psyche was once again called upon to create someone who could live above the turmoil.

Sadly, my young-adult self was created with a belief about who she was that never before existed. This would cause me to make decisions very different from my child and teen selves. These decisions would eventually lead me to the cliff where I attempted suicide at twenty three—then quickly repressed the memory.

From college to the cliff, no matter what happened, there was a determination to live above the trauma and pain. I did enjoy life—though not with the same abandon as in my teen years. Dorm life was enjoyable most of the time, and lifelong friendships were built. My passion for working with young children was born during those years, leading me to accept positions in early childhood centers and eventually, at the age of twenty two, to be hired as the director of a preschool.

During college in San Diego, it was necessary to be successful academically and also to care for Jane. This was accomplished by creating a "student skill alter" who could sit in the library and do homework for ten-hour stretches. She was destined for Ph.D. work! She spent Saturdays in the library completing all homework for the week without distractions—trust me, no one else was in the library! This lessened the stress while attending classes. On Sunday, my time was free to sit by the marina, go to an organ concert in Balboa Park, or walk on the beach.

The human spirit is truly remarkable. I figured out what my life was supposed to look like and marched toward it. By studying psychology and child development, my subconscious understood much of the truth about myself, but it didn't fit the life I wanted to live. My choice to become a professional in the field of early childhood came from my belief in the importance of early wiring.

During the years when I should have been developing my adult identity, my attempts to overcome the trauma of my childhood were met by the deepest types of betrayal. But those sad tales will never be told. The days when depression and despair drowned me are too numerous to wrap my mind around. What is remarkable is how my decimated being kept getting up day after day and giving life one more try.

OVER COFFEE

Two years after entering therapy, I was having coffee with a friend who knew my story.

"So, how are you with cliffs now?" she asked.

I grabbed my jacket and wrapped it tightly around me. Disturbed by the intensity of my reaction, I wondered. *I am well now, aren't I?*

I had recently ended therapy. My new level of independence made it seem unnecessary. Of course, the door was always open to return. But everything in me cried "No!" as I attempted to wrap my jacket tightly around my soul.

Will my issues with the cliff ever end?

That night in my dreams, I saw a girl running—running to a stand of trees along a gravel path. She wasn't a child, but she wasn't an adult either. She was some part of me, but I had no memory of running like that since childhood.

"Call Dr. Sue," Scott said.

My mind considered this, but at what point did I just need to take care of my*self*?

"If we move, as we've been thinking about doing, I'll be too far away from Dr. Sue. I need to see if I can take care of myself."

My healing self wanted to figure it out on my own.

Typing on my phone, which sometimes helped find a memory, the running girl returned to talk to me. She was my college-freshman self.

"What happened to you?" I asked, "Why did you change? You seemed fine when you went to college, but something changed."

It was a relatively warm day and she wanted to go to the picnic area in the Garden of the Gods. She wanted to be able to walk after she told her story. We had been to the spot often.

Settled at a picnic table, eating my packed lunch, a sudden chill came over me as a cloud bank rolled in and forced me to move back to the car. The memory was coming. Surfacing memories felt familiar by this time. I wondered if typing the story might help.

What my fingers typed was raw and graphic. This is my retelling:

I was a freshman in college and had gone home for Thanksgiving. My mother, without consulting with me, had agreed for me to go on a date with a son of one of the church members—whom I had briefly met the summer before and instantly disliked. Putting on the skirt, blouse, and sweater she thought I should wear, I went without argument—it just wasn't worth fighting with her.

Thinking we were going out to eat, the direction he drove didn't make sense. He said he wanted to show me the river first. Despite expressing my lack of interest in this idea, he was not deterred and we careened down country roads to the riverbank, where he parked and began to grope me.

I tried to protect myself by wrapping my sweater tightly around me. I managed to get out of the car door and run—but not fast enough. What happened in the next half hour was violent, disgusting, and terrifying. Through my dissociative fog I heard him say, "You really liked this, didn't you?"

As usual, I developed a "cover story" in which I was brave and strong and told him, "No!" and made him drive away from the riverbank. In my perfect story, he took me to eat with a friend at a truck stop and then took me home. This was all true—with the violence tidily repressed.

What really happened at the truck stop was he introduced me to his friend by saying, "This is Janyne, and you're really going to like her."

Back in the car, tightly crammed between them—and being groped—the car careened across intersections, ignoring stop signs, and headed far into the country again. I was thrown in the backseat and raped again, but the raw pain prevented me from dissociating. My screams echoed into the unhearing darkness.

As he straightened my clothes, brushed the leaves from my hair, and tidied my sweater around my now-buttoned blouse, he said, "You won't tell anyone about this, because if you do, I will tell them the preacher's slut daughter came to town and she wanted this." Finally, they took me home. My only memory was that of careening down dark country roads.

The next day, while in the kitchen with my mother, the phone rang. She answered it and handed it to me, saying his name (which I don't recall).

He said, "I want you to sit next to me at church tomorrow. Everyone knows we went on a date, and you don't want anyone to think anything bad happened, right?"

I hung up the phone.

"You didn't say anything. Did he want you to go out with him again? If so, you should go. You could go out tonight."

I felt all the pressure that had made me go on the date in the first place. I sensed her wanting to impress the prominent church family with their daughter who was home from college. The disgust I had felt for him even before I went was intense. I remembered the warning signs I had to ignore because to battle my mother wouldn't have been worth it. I remembered regretting I had allowed my mother to make me wear a skirt in order to look nice for dinner.

Suppressing my urge to scream, I answered, "No mother. He just said he would see me in church tomorrow."

"Well, you did behave yourself last night, didn't you?"

I felt my anger. I felt my rage. I felt my insides where I had been torn.

"Why would you say that?"

"Well, you always have thrown yourself at the men."

I was dazed. There was just nothing in my 'I had one boyfriend and we were good' life which caused her to say this. My subconscious, repressed memories of repeated sexual abuse must have been screaming.

I exploded. "That is not true! Why would you say that to me?"

To which she replied, "Well it has been who you are ever since you were very little."

The dark clouds above the Garden of the Gods now shrouded

the car where I was sitting with my computer in my lap. The memory shook and convulsed from my body as my fingers typed. Looking back at what had been typed, there were places where my fingers had gotten on the wrong keys and typed gibberish, but most of what was there would have been worthy of a porn novel.

The final sentence and the blankness of the page underneath it felt much like my dead soul. My world reeled about me as a blue jay landed in front of me and appeared to be concerned.

I screamed, "Who I was since I was little?"

The words hung in the car.

Like a blanket of shame, my mother's rejection of me when I was abused at three, her refusal to ever hold me or touch me again unless necessary, the constant distrust of me without cause, and her ever-present judgment landed on top of me with a smothering reality.

Amidst ravaging sobs I cried, "That's not who I was!"

The parking lot emptied as if to honor the grief beginning to explode out of me. The replay of my life moved forward from that evening by the river. The person who emerged was never the same as before. After that, painful situations would trap me again and again. All the bad choices I made—ignoring inner warnings, not removing myself from damaging situations— now made sense. What I believed about myself shifted away from the child who firmly believed the bad things done to her were not her fault. Instead, I came to believe it *was* my fault— because of "who I had been since I was very little"—someone who pushed herself on men. My heart was wrenched. Eventually I would create Non Janyne to control this evil lie that took residence inside of me.

Alone in my car, it no longer seemed a good idea to try to

process this memory on my own. But with the memory now so clear, surely it was possible to walk through the aftermath.... *Walking—that's what I need!*

I drove further into the park, parked my car in an unfamiliar place, and began to walk. I dodged tourists while giving Scott a call (which was a bit incoherent and troubling to him). Climbing a set of stairs, I found myself inside a formation that looked oddly like The Cave of Memories.

I sat there for some time before returning to my car to drive home. I felt better. But I called Dr. Sue to tell her about the memory that had surfaced and which I was convinced I had now processed.

Getting Lost

About a week later, still thinking the college-freshman memory had been successfully processed, I learned one final lesson about how unprocessed pain surfaces in very inconvenient ways.

I was doing well and felt grounded—most of the time. My only lingering frustration was driving. The anxiety involved in getting into my car and driving across town was growing inexplicably worse instead of better. Then I got lost.

Winter would soon arrive, but it was a perfect seventy-five degree day. Heading for Garden of the Gods to walk in the sunshine, I parked my car in the unfamiliar spot I had found a few days earlier. I started my walk with hopes of making a new memory. I guess I accomplished that goal.

What happened was clearly a demonstration of the compartmentalization in my dissociative brain. One "me" parked the car and headed out, only to reach a place where another "me" normally walked. I shifted, then, and finished my walk as the second person. The one who had found the parking spot the first day was seventeen. The one who normally walks in the park was sixty three—and thought she was done shifting.

The seventeen-year-old headed "south" (really north) on a path she had never seen (a familiar path for the adult). She spotted the Kissing Camels rock formation and suddenly the sixty-three year old knew where she was and took over—leaving the location of my car in another part of my brain. North was south and south was north. In my mind the rock structure of Kissing Camels could only be viewed from the East. The fact that the seventeen year old saw it from the west side was a fact that the division in my brain completely blocked.

At one point during my three miles of walking in search of my car, the car was in view and could have been seen, but my brain would not allow it. The adult me knew exactly where I was, but the teenager was careening down country roads losing all sense of direction and thought she was in danger.

Finally, I sat on a rock and called Scott, asking him to come get me.

"Do you know where you are?"

Well, yes, but the location of my car was a mystery. It did no good to stare at the maps, since my brain would not allow me to see the path to my car. It was like a movie where someone finds a town, but when she goes back it isn't there. I was alone in the midst of hundreds of tourists and terrified. Left was right and right was left. It never occurred to me that Kissing Camels could be seen from either side of the rock formation.

Like a lost hitchhiker, I stood at the edge of the road and waited for Scott to rescue me. We drove around a curve and there was my bright red car—right where the teenager had left it.

The car was found. But my mind was still split between my teen and adult selves. The wrong one showed up to have coffee with a friend the next day. My friend didn't understand. And neither did I—except that the need for therapy was quite obvious.

I made an appointment with Dr. Sue, sat on the couch, and entered the memory.

> *"I don't know where I am. The car is going too fast. He isn't taking me to dinner. I don't want to go to the river. He scares me. I don't know where we are. I am trying to read the road signs, but he is going too fast. We are turning. Left, then right; no, then left; no, right. I can never keep it straight. I will never find my way back. What if he leaves me out here?"*

There it was—the connection between the memory, the anxiety in driving, and losing my car in the park.

"This is exactly how it feels in my car. Why would it seem so confusing on such familiar roads? It was terrifying. That is also how I felt in the park. I could not remember if I had gone left or right. The map made no sense. The adult me was there, too; but the seventeen year old couldn't tell me where the car was."

Being split in two parts at the same time with this degree of disconnect was a new experience for me. Not even when the Three Chairs were in control had I felt this way. They shifted, but didn't try to occupy at the same time! It occurred to me The Watcher (a gatekeeper in my system, which I haven't fully detailed in this book) controlled the shifting and was effective in avoiding these dissociative moments.

I didn't ever want it to happen again. But this experience was informative. It seemed EMDR processing could prevent these episodes. Yes, the memory had surfaced, but it had not been completely processed. Lesson learned.

Scott and I went back and walked the paths to help me put

the two sides of my brain back together. The two sides of rock formations had been placed in completely different areas in my brain. Only a few steps more in various spots could have connected the two, but it was as if an invisible wall kept me back. This was probably the clearest example of compartmentalization experienced during my journey.

Later, my friend and I laughed about our inexplicable conversation over coffee.

"Janyne, we just could not connect with each other."

No, something had been horribly wrong. My teen self was begging for help and needed me to listen to her and help her find her way to safety. When I had repressed the painful memory, I had left her out on the dark road trying to figure out how to get back home. After I returned to therapy and completely processed the memory, the driving anxiety started to diminish.

This memory of what happened at the river—and of the conversation with my mother the next day—provided the reason for the deep distress I felt later, on the cliff.

FORESHADOWING THE CLIFF

There was something about cliffs. "I feel like I'm falling off a cliff," was how I described my darkest days, even before beginning therapy. I didn't feel as though I was jumping but, instead, falling with my face to the cliff. This didn't make sense.

When I didn't sign the contract for another year at my faculty position, I had described it as leaping off a cliff. It appeared leaping was intentional while falling was not. On a whim, I searched for the word "cliff" on my computer, and hundreds of files, documents, and emails appeared. Evidently, cliffs were a big deal to me.

My ever-present fear of heights and mountain roads was inconvenient since we lived at the foot of the Rocky Mountains.

Not to be denied the experience, I took the cog railway to the top of Pikes Peak but could not bring myself to look over the edge except from inside the rail car.

My fear of mountain roads had been palpable all during therapy. Dr. Sue only had to mention driving in the mountains or looking over a cliff, and my reaction made it clear there was something.... We just couldn't find it.

Only two memories were connected to mountain roads. The first had occured when I was about seven and my family drove the newly-paved road up to Sandia Crest. My brother and I got out of the car and ran up the steps toward the lookout. My mother was screaming at us to stop as we jostled up the stairway. I have always remembered crawling to the edge to look over. Apparently she instilled fear in me.

The other memory took place during a trip with my parents when I was a young adult. We drove over a winding pass somewhere in the Rocky Mountains while my mother screeched in the front seat.

I cowered in the back seat, unable to look over the side.

My father said, "Myrtle, if I was going any slower, I would be stopped."

As soon as we reached the hotel I went to bed, sick with fear.

Yes, it was fear, but it seemed the fear had existed before this trip and was much more intense than what my child self felt when she crawled to the edge to look over. We just could not find the root memory.

"When we get to where you think you would be able, we will take a drive up in the mountains," said Dr. Sue.

I agreed, because an adventure sounded fun. But I doubted a day would exist when the fear would subside enough to make this possible.

Then we found the cliff.

FINALLY

During the second summer of therapy, Scott and I took a trip to California to connect with our daughter and take the grandkids to Disneyland. As we drove along the foothills above L.A., while I was looking up something on my phone, a small gray truck moved into our lane and sideswiped us. We were traveling at 70 mph, but Scott veered into the wide median and navigated off the freeway and into the gravel.

When the car stopped, I jumped out screaming, "I didn't die! I didn't die!"

It was overly dramatic, but I couldn't stop shaking and running. Where? It wasn't clear. Finally I realized we were both fine and the car was drivable. So we continued on our trip, but I had an uneasy feeling my reaction was an indicator a memory was trying to surface. This was exactly the case.

Back home, while caring for my grandkids, who had come to stay with us, the memory began to download. It took several sessions to fully understand what had taken me to the cliff—a betrayal so profound, in fact, that it will never be told.

The memories of the cliff were processed over a tortuous, several-week period. Sometime later, I wrote the following piece. It is a summary of the events and place of healing I came to, but it does not portray the deep trauma or despair that took me to the cliff.

WHEN GOD IS NOT IN CONTROL[1]

"I don't have choices."

The words hung in the air. Through almost two years of therapy, Dr. Sue and I had struggled to find a source for this deep-seated belief. My story of repressed childhood sexual abuse would have predicated anything but a successful life, and yet I had a Ph.D., professional career, and a thirty-eight-year marriage. I obviously had made choices (good ones). Yet, again I had said I did not have choices. Where was this faulty belief buried?

Then, as a result of a car accident on an L.A. freeway, the memory of skidding out on a mountain road surfaced.

"I didn't die, I didn't die," I had screamed as I ran from the car, not knowing where I was running to.

Now I know that I was looking for the cliff that I had run to forty years earlier—the cliff where I tried to end my life after a betrayal so deep I couldn't recover.

That day so long ago, as my car skidded and I ran to stand on the edge of the cliff, a man had stopped to help me. Obviously skilled, he convinced me to turn and step back. But the dirt crumbled beneath my feet. I slid off the cliff and clung to a tree root until he rescued me.

As I lay on the dirt, I believed God had stopped me from ending my life. I believed the choice to end the pain had been taken from me. I had been taught God was always in control. The only way I could make sense of my life was to believe that God had allowed the abuse, and now he had stopped me from stepping off the cliff.

Why would God stop *me* but not all the others who succeeded in ending their lives? Did he love me more? Was he trying to build character through the trauma I had experienced? Did he have some great purpose I had not yet fulfilled?

Every morning for forty years, as I emerged from sleep, I reenacted the fall from the cliff in a symbolic feeling of dread. My hands never relaxed. On dark days I would say, "I feel like I am falling off a cliff."

I was trying to express the reality I had repressed.

Buried with the repressed memory was the reason I believed I did not have choices—it was all about theology.

After I was coaxed back to my car, the man sat beside me and asked, "Do you believe in God?"

Oddly enough, I said, "I believe God loves me." The broken child in me never doubted God's love.

But how could I reconcile that love with the life I had lived? During two years of intensive therapy, the pain had exploded out of my soul. I was three… I was six… I was nine… I was twelve… I was fourteen. Finally, as a young adult I concluded that God loved me but didn't protect me when he could have. And he made me live when I wanted to die. How could I make sense of it all?

"What is your anchor, Janyne?" Dr. Sue had asked.

In my mind, I was in a lake of pain about to be sucked into a whirlpool. "I know I'm supposed to say God. I know you want me to say God. But no, God is not my anchor."

The words spoken from a couple dozen fractured parts of me hung between us. If God could prevent pain, then why didn't he?

It would be months before I understood I did have choices. I finally realized I could not accept I had choices because I could not accept the fact that those who hurt me also had choices. It was all about free will. If I could choose, then they could choose, and God really was not controlling the situation. If God wasn't in control, then he did not save me from stepping off the cliff, and there was not some great purpose I needed to fulfill … and I wasn't sure I wanted to live. This was something my theology would not allow me to process.

I drove down the mountain by following the taillights of the man God had sent to keep me alive. I felt like George in the movie *It's a Wonderful Life*. God had chosen for me to live, and I needed to live a life worthy of his choosing. I let others make choices for me; I believed what they wanted me to believe. I became a theological chameleon and buried my pain so deeply, it didn't erupt until I turned sixty one. I did live a wonderful life, but I was never able to truly worship the God who I believed chose to make me live but did not protect me.

The day I realized I had choices was the day I understood God was not a controlling God. He did not control me on the cliff; I chose to turn and live. I chose, but so did all those who hurt me. We all had free will. I didn't need to say nonsensical things such as, "God allowed my abuse in order to build character."

He felt sorrow, he comforted me, and he prompted me to seek help; but I made the choices.

"Janyne, do you believe you have choices?" Dr. Sue asked me again.

"Yes, I do believe I have choices because I believe God loves me and as a result he has given me free will. He has given everyone free will; he will not coercively stop human choices, be they for good or for evil. He will seek to influence for good. But everyone makes their own choices."

I believe that outside of an understanding of an uncontrolling God, there is no potential for truly transcending the human experience of trauma, living life abundantly, and worshipping freely. The God who controls could not be my anchor, but the God who loves me, comforts me, brings me support by prompting the actions of others, and guides my choices most certainly can!

---

1. This section (slightly edited for this book), with its account of what happened on the cliff, was originally written as an essay published as a guest post on the blog "Uncontrolling Love." It may be accessed at http://uncontrollinglove.com/2016/11/10/when-god-is-not-in-control/. This marked the first time I shared any part of my story in a public venue—a brave but terrifying step! The essay has since been published in the book compilation, *Uncontrolling Love: Conversations on the Love of God*, edited by Thomas Jay Oord (2017, SacraSage Press).

Gold Camp Road

We had "found" the cliff, and it finally made sense. My fear of mountain roads had a reason. It was time to take therapy off the couch and into the world. We had worked through numerous levels of this memory over several weeks before we were confident about the benefit of taking a drive on a mountain road.

My fear had certainly not vanished. As we headed toward the mountains, I asked, "Where are we going?"

"I thought I would take you on Gold Camp Road." Dr. Sue said.

I was stunned. It was a road that had originally been a track for the trains to bring gold over the mountain to the smelter. (Later when I told my son where we went, he—like everyone familiar with it—understood it was significant.) My body braced.

At one point the paved road changes to a dirt road. I felt the scream begin inside of me but contained it. To my relief, there was a turnout ahead.

"Pull over! I need you to pull over!!"

She pulled over.

Sitting in the turnout, I tried to regain my composure. I looked above me and saw a cliff very similar to the one where I slipped.

"The dirt road was the trigger!" I exclaimed.

Pulling off the pavement in LA had been the trigger also. The week before, Scott and I had taken a wrong turn and ended up on a dirt road—and I panicked. Changing from pavement to dirt had always been an issue. It always felt out of control. Sliding on ice had the same feeling—it wasn't the ice, it was this feeling.

"We can turn around here, Janyne. It is your choice. If you don't think you are ready, that's fine. If you think you can, we can continue. It's your choice." She watched me carefully.

I pondered. What if we turned back? Shame was a possibility, but we could work through it. No, this was basically fear, and the transition to the dirt road was a trigger. It might not be enjoyable, but it was possible.

"Tell me what is ahead. It will be better if I know what is coming."

"We will continue on this dirt road for about ten minutes. There will be two tunnels to go through. Then we will get back to pavement and go down the hill to Helen Hunt Falls. We can stop there if you like, or we can go sit at the creek and process."

"OK," I said in my most unconvincing voice.

My eyes were glued to the front of the car as we continued, never looking to the left or the right. My body did manage to relax and enjoy the tunnel. My relief was evident when we reached the creek. We waded into the water and sat on rocks. The cold water was calming.

We repeated the drive two more times. In between, we went to the couch and processed additional surfacing memories. On the second drive, I looked around but without enjoyment. The third time, the view was much more enjoyable, and we even got out and looked over the side into the canyon below. The children did ask Dr. Sue to hold their hands. Being an adult was often lost on them. It was OK. I was willing to do whatever these child selves needed to feel safe while the adult me tried to heal.

Slowly the memory of the cliff began to lose its grip on me. I stopped climbing up over the cliff every morning when I awoke. My processing helped me to understand how the cliff experience had so profoundly changed my life. It was there that Non Janyne was created and she would control me for the next forty years. She believed, as my mother had told me, that what happened to me before driving to the cliff was all because of *who I was*—who I had been since I was little.

CONTINUING TO MAKE SENSE OF THE CLIFF

The pieces of my life were finally making sense. My seemingly random reactions to so many things did have causes. I didn't become a lover of mountain roads like my therapist who appeared to be part mountain goat, but my pathological fear, that kept me from enjoying the mountains, was almost gone.

An interesting piece connected to the cliff had occurred during the autumn before the cliff memory surfaced. On a lovely fall day in the desert, Scott and I had taken the morning to enjoy a hiking trail up the side of a mountain in Scottsdale. Climbing the rocky path, I sensed going up was much easier than coming back down would be.

Sure enough. We reached a stopping point, marveled at the desert view, took pictures and turned to go back down. I started shaking and had to sit on a rock.

"Give me a minute. It appears to be trauma releasing."

Since so much healing had taken place, this problem surprised us. Gathering up courage to walk, I said, "What we have to do is you walk in front of me and I will follow you. Go slowly, please."

And we were off ... slowly, very slowly. We kept "pulling over" to allow others to pass—while my body shook uncontrollably. Then a woman about my age, extremely agile and confident, passed us, almost running down the mountain.

I thought, *That is me! What am I doing creeping down this hill?*

Scott watched in shock as I took off around him and began to run down the rocky path. He caught up with me at the bottom of the hill.

"What was that?" he asked. "Did you shift?"

"I don't know. But it would appear I did." So confusing!

Almost a year later, when my cliff memory surfaced, and I remembered driving down the hill behind the man in his car, I realized that memory fit on top of this strange episode of my suddenly running down the hiking trail, like a fitted sheet. It was clearly a PTSD reenactment. On the way down the hill after my suicide attempt, as I was repressing the memory, I suddenly had no idea why I was following a slow-moving car. I sped up and passed him and never looked back—or remembered.

I did wonder, that day after the suicide attempt, why my dress was dirty and torn. I threw it away and then kept searching for it. I also wondered what happened to my parking brake, which never held tight after that day. My recurring nightmare was of being in a car headed for a cliff and desperately trying to press the brake pedal (which I now understand was the clutch).

MAKING SENSE OF MYSELF

It was all beginning to make sense!

My child self had been blessed with an unbelievably strong core and sense of self. Even at three, she knew she deserved to live a life despite the pain. That small child marched through life with determination. At every age, I simply got up and kept fighting. The effort would eventually take its toll; but even as I healed, strength and tenacity would continue to propel me.

My structures were functional. Few would have ever known the truth of my story. Why not stop pushing and step quietly into retirement?

Was it necessary to pursue every avenue and turn every stone? Maybe it would have been possible to finish my life without ever releasing the carefully guarded pain. Maybe.

The problem was that, from the youngest age my child selves had been trying to make sense to themselves. My determination to understand myself showed up in all my educational and career paths. I was never going to be satisfied with anything less than complete understanding. There would be no resting until the answers embedded in my story were found. I needed to make sense to myself.

Despite this longing, I also needed to live out my adult life, hold my marriage intact, raise my children, and complete my career before opening the door to my mind. Once opened, there was no going back. I needed to bring resolution to every inexplicable part of my life.

18
Adult Years

That terrible day on the cliff changed everything. Janyne, Jane, and Non Janyne were created that day as the perfect adult system. The Three Chairs, with the aid of The Watcher, would successfully orchestrate my life for decades. While the children held triggers that affected my life, they were tightly controlled and seldom shifted in uncontrollable ways.

This does not discount the fact that there were three adults, two young adults, two teens, five sets of twins, a three year old, and The Watcher compartmentalized in my psyche. Although my dissociative system enabled me to accomplish much, it also resulted in my living just outside the abundant, joyful life that should have been mine to live. Though I never could access abundance and joy, I fought every day to get as close to them as possible.

SEEING MY INNER WORLD

It took two years of therapy to find all the parts of my dissociative system—assuming we *had* found them all. At this point, it is not my intent to discuss the structure of dissociative systems, but I do want to emphasize that how the mind organizes this particular form of coping mechanism should be understood as a system. There are typical roles and parts in almost all systems. I purposefully did not do research before I identified the parts of my system, and when I did, it was uncanny to see the similarities. My particular system is complex but not chaotic—in fact, it is inherently beautiful and strong, and I will fully describe and explain it in the sequel to this book.

The system that developed was clearly built upon the subconscious need to split in order to hold the extensive pain and was the result of the creative genius of a child. Each child was a distinct personality with a role to play, forming a rich inner landscape. Splitting was a cognitive coping strategy designed to help me live life. It succeeded, but with quirks and glitches everyone assumed were just uniquely me—and they were!

Uncovering the system was a treasure trove of sense making, but reliving the abuse that caused the splitting, in order to heal, was wrenching. The well of repressed pain I held inside my body was terrifying and felt endless. My life was affected every day in complex ways. Once revealed, the system provided insights as to how I successfully functioned during my adult years.

LIVING WITH TRIGGERS

It should not have been possible to live my adult years without apparent dysfunction resulting from such extensive trauma. During therapy, we processed an astounding number of triggers. Non Janyne was the one who had the power to walk through triggers. Triggers caused me to involuntarily shift and relive the emotions of trauma without knowing the cause. Before I was able to heal the cause of the trigger during therapy, it was necessary to control (or hide) the reactions. Without control, my life would have looked like a pinball game in which I bounced from one uncontrolled behavior to another.

My ability to control triggers enabled me to live a functional life—but one fraught with anxiety and panic attacks. The list of triggers seemed endless: waiting my turn, handshakes, arched eyebrows, fear of getting lost, being shushed, cleaning a bathtub, having my feet trapped, snowy days, dirt roads, Brussels sprouts ... on and on it goes. The causes are now understood. With the attached experiences now healed, I have cognitive knowledge of the triggers, but I rarely have emotional reactions.

Being able to control triggers kept me from shifting in unrestrained ways. As my structures began to come apart, though, and The Watcher's role weakened, the triggers began to shift me without warning. Without controls in place to keep this from happening, I began to catch a glimpse of how chaotic my entire adult life might have been. One example of this came the time I lost the location of my car in another part of my brain.

Control kept me from living in chaos. Not all are so fortunate or strong. Their uncontrolled and inexplicable reactions to triggers become fodder for ridicule. This causes re-traumatization of the traumatized. There is much we should not judge.

At times I could not control a trigger. My reaction was a bit odd, but my self-defense mechanisms were ready and waiting. People seemed to love my self-deprecating humor. Sometimes the oddness was merely being human (like everyone else); but sometimes, it was a shift or a temporary dissociation.

My determination to live life is probably most remarkable when considering triggers. As the memories surfaced and the triggers and shifting ran rampant, I was frightened to find myself in uncontrollable fear and chaos. My fear of my own inner self was not unfounded. My belief that Jane could have imploded my life was certainly correct. My jubilation on the day I "finished well" and retired was deserved.

My newfound appreciation for my dissociative system, and

how it allowed me to live life and raise my family, is also correctly placed. My faith in God to one day bring me healing was based on a subconscious understanding of the depth of my pain and the dysfunction it had created.

With healing, triggers lost their power and the tight control became less necessary. Without healing, control was the only answer. Control was how I lived my life. Now I understand why I chose to do things the ways I did. I thought it was just part of my personality. In some ways it was, but how I accomplished what I needed to do every day was not "normal" in any sense of the word. It just looked normal—most of the time.

How I lived as Janyne, Non Janyne, and Jane is a book unto itself and provides many illustrations for how I lived within my dissociative system and hid it so effectively. If my healing journey had only focused on the adult symptoms, I would not be where I am today. The adult who went to therapy, got exposed in EMDR therapy, and said, "Which One?" was well versed in hiding behind a mask of being completely "normal." It is no wonder dissociation is so difficult to diagnose!

Part III
BREATHING

My experience on the cliff ended the experiences of trauma. I came down the hill in three parts ready to live my adult life. Externally, I would live my life as if no childhood trauma had occurred. I would only partially understand those things that occurred in my young adult life. After the cliff experience, which I immediately repressed, there were many incorrect interpretations and survival strategies, but no additional trauma. The subconscious goal of the Three Chairs was to effectively live the life of someone who had never experienced trauma.

The life I lived was not *despite* being dissociative; it was *because* I was dissociative. Splitting off parts enabled me to live above the pain and accomplish my dreams.

I consider myself fortunate. Many family members, friends, teachers, counselors, and even students may have caught a glimpse of Jane and the children along the way, but they loved and cared about me in ways that helped me survive—and outwardly thrive. God cared for me through them, and I always believed healing would one day come.

God's guidance, love, and care during the healing process was evident. Healing has come! Now I can finally breathe! The joy and abundance I desired is mine.

19
The Curriculum

My understanding of God's working in the world has been altered as a result of my healing journey. The Blueprint idea of God being in control and pre-planning every detail of my life has been completely obliterated. Holding to this belief would mean that abuse was part of God's plan—but it was not. This does not negate God's intimate involvement in my journey. It also does not change the truth of God stepping into my life and directing me in choices, which if ignored, would hinder living out the adventure God desired for me. My choices made a difference. Our choices *make* a difference.

My understanding of God's incredible power in the events of our lives has expanded exponentially—but in ways that emphasize relationship. God's prompting and guidance, which will be shared in this chapter, were absolutely essential, but so were my decisions to listen, respond, and act. The God who loves me and desires healing never forced me to take a single step. Nor did God force Dr. Sue to care for me in ways beyond professional or personal expectation. Likewise, God did not force Scott to calmly support his wife when she had clearly fallen down a rabbit hole.

My healing is miraculous. But even a miracle requires human cooperation. If you decide to cooperate, watch out because God's curriculum will take you where you never imagined! For me it was somewhat like Dorothy following the yellow brick road to the Emerald City. I never knew what I would find around the next turn. I just kept taking the next step and following the path.

How To Heal a Dissociative Disorder

The human soul desires and pursues wholeness. All my inner structures were built to emulate a whole, healthy human. I studied psychology and understood all the characteristics of wholeness and did everything in my power to be that image. It was a lonesome internal journey.

Healing was also a lonely journey; but from the very beginning, I knew that I had a support team. The role my husband and therapist played in my healing has been obvious. I could not have healed alone. But there was one more participant—God. We called God's plan for my healing, "The Curriculum." My responsibility was to follow it step by step.

Step 1: Listen for God's Prompting

How does one heal a dissociative disorder? Find an extremely qualified and dedicated therapist. In my case, God completed this task for me. My belief in God's clear presence and prompting to make the appointment with a specific therapist steadied me when doubts consumed me. For some reason, God speaks most clearly to me in my car, but you should not wait to hear the prompting in a car, OK? God prompts in so many ways.

My story convinces me that when a person needs a therapist, it is possible to be guided to the right one. Researching is a good plan. If you know trauma is part of the story, there are therapists who are specifically trained in this area.

I, of course, would recommend you find a therapist with EMDR training. God desires healing and uses many avenues. If you also desire healing, God will guide you!

All my determination would have been useless without Dr. Sue. She doesn't want me to say this. She wants to give me credit for my own healing, because she knows how hard and bravely I worked. She also knows that without Scott's support, she could not have provided care to the extent needed. We were all a team, but in a myriad of ways my healing came down to one skilled and caring therapist. She will just have to accept that acknowledgment, because without her skill and care this story could have ended tragically.

First, Dr. Sue's goal was to help the child inside of me heal. We didn't initially know there were multiple children, but the healing process was still the same. My problems manifested in adult ways, but they were not adult problems. Various behavior-focused therapies can be effective in changing adult behaviors, but transformation is dependent on healing the inner child. Only then can we unwind the causes for our often-debilitating emotions and behaviors. She worked to help heal every child who appeared. They sat on hands, told her they didn't trust her, tried to run from therapy, called her in desperation, and asked her to hug them. She demonstrated how to care for each of them and, in so doing, taught me how to care for myself.

Second, Dr. Sue trusted my intuition. My ability to actually see and analyze my inner structures was a gift to both of us. Added to this was my uncanny ability to take apparently unconnected memories and make connections that took us exactly where we needed to go.

Between sessions I spent entire days processing. Upon returning to therapy, I was light years from where I had been when the previous session ended. She trusted me to know where we needed to go next, and she trusted herself to know how to support me. I would often send her an email to catch her up before the session so we could move directly to what we needed to address. What often felt like an imposition on her time was always greeted with gratitude for communicating so we both understood where we were headed.

Third, Dr. Sue listened to her own intuition. Sometimes it was merely a well-placed inquiry or prompt, but other times she was willing to take therapy off the couch and into the world. Our mountain drives, which helped me process the cliff memory, are the most obvious examples. In my case, this was necessary because there were memories and parts of the dissociative system that were never going to fully surface without real-world experiences. Some alters lived in the world and never entered the therapy office.

When children appeared, I usually wasn't aware of the shifting. She moved into the conversation with the child in ways that kept me safe. The most unexpected shift was when she placed the "mother doll" in the chair for me to speak to as if she were my mother. My shift to a six year old, and the ensuing dramatic reaction, was something we will never forget. To our surprise, I collapsed into incoherent terror because of the doll's arched eyebrow!

My dissociative episodes of staring were met with a calm, steady gaze of assurance. When shame attacked, she never allowed me to walk away with it. Yes, both intuitively and professionally, she always understood what healing required on any particular day. It was rare that we weren't on the same page—and this was usually the result of my own tendency toward projection.

Fourth and finally, Dr. Sue was "all in"—completely dedicated. Healing dissociative disorders is complex and time consuming. My disorder involved abandonment, insecure attachment, and dependency issues. When shifting occurred multiple times in a session, staying within the time frame of a one-hour session was challenging no matter how hard I tried. (It didn't help when children appeared and they could not read the time on the analog clock, or know how to drive home.) Extended sessions, self-care panic calls, and phone sessions were given with the utmost professionalism and care—all the while leading me to independence by providing the security I needed.

I was always determined to work harder than Dr. Sue was working, but she always gave more than I could have paid or asked for. What we did was a team effort. My willingness to do whatever it took to heal made it possible for her to invest in me in ways that were above and beyond professional expectations. I understand and am overwhelmed by what she chose to do.

STEP 2: FOLLOW THE CURRICULUM

The Curriculum could probably fill another book (what a great idea!). Sometimes I would try to slow down but would suddenly be plummeted into another memory. This usually occurred as the result of some random event in my life. The trick was to not miss the importance of what seemed random.

It was necessary to listen to my feelings—not a strong skill for me. I had to learn to ask myself, "What is that feeling? What is surfacing? What is it that causes me to feel this way?"

The most obvious examples of unexplainable feelings were my fear of heights and mountain roads, and my endless references to the cliff. Dr. Sue sensed the importance of my references to falling off cliffs early in our sessions. Her skill in sensing my feelings was essential, but my ability to listen to my own feelings developed slowly. Listening to my feelings usually required help, and that was often fulfilled by The Curriculum. The odd situations in which I found myself, and the ways in which these situations caused memories to surface, often caused the *Twilight Zone* theme to play in my head.

The emotional clues were usually triggers such as handshakes, Brussels sprouts, dirt roads, etc. Sometimes the memory that surfaced was completely unexpected—such as the time I found myself face to face with a roadrunner. The roadrunner experience, and many others, provided a path to healing, and they will be told in my forthcoming book about the "children."

For me, the most remarkable part of The Curriculum was the odd assortment of things I had carefully carried with me through my life. Like Gretel, I had dropped breadcrumbs for myself. Most of these items had been kept since childhood. It seemed my subconscious was collecting clues to help me when the time came to unravel the story.

I would say, "I think there is something in a box."

With a smile Dr. Sue would respond, "Of course there is!"

Trips were also an essential part of The Curriculum. I love travelling and seeing family and friends, but this was not the true purpose of the trips. Travelling made me try out healing plateaus. Travelling made me feel somewhat normal. Travelling also brought memories to the surface.

Every trip took me back to therapy. We all began to recognize this as part of the process. From the car accident to hearing the lonely sound of a train whistle on a Kansas plain, I was led toward additional layers needing to be healed. The amount of traveling during my second year of therapy was ridiculous. It seemed impossible to stay out of planes. My Facebook followers thought it was a game of "Where in the World is Janyne?" I longed for the day when a trip did not send me back to therapy—and it did finally happen.

We all felt God weaving The Curriculum throughout my journey. Even my father, who almost lived to be 101, unknowingly dropped clues until the week before he died. I became accustomed to how memories surfaced, and I developed a heightened sense of awareness of God's promptings—often through nature. Even in the most difficult times of processing, God's presence comforted me during and after therapy.

We never doubted The Curriculum. Without my determination to listen, I would have missed so much God was trying to reveal to me. God couldn't force it into my head; I had to be willing to listen, look for the clues, step into the experiences, and believe I would come out on the other side.

My belief in God's presence and working resided in my child self. Religious dogma and trappings, though present in my adult world, were not the basis for my faith. When all was stripped from me and the hollow religious answers held no value, my childlike relationship with God held me tightly. That God loved me and desired to heal me was all that really mattered.

STEP 3: BE WILLING TO GO DEEP

Processing repressed memories, emotions, and messages requires intensive work. Willingness to reach the deepest, most painful experiences is essential. This requires determination since the mind is often resolute in not allowing the uncovering.

Part of this uncovering was finding the incorrect messages embedded in me as a child. These messages ran through my daily life like well-rehearsed scripts. Everyone has scripts from childhood. They are meant to be affirmations of our worth and importance. Some of mine were—but then there were the others that told me things about myself that were simply not true. While developing a sense of self, the messages of abuse and the voice of my mother embedded many unfounded beliefs about myself.

I had always sensed the importance of childhood messages, and my interest in teaching math came mainly from trying to help students overcome the messages they had received as children. Mathematics provides much fodder for buried messages. It was astounding how many adults explained that their parents told them not to worry about math, because they couldn't ever do math either. This was actually more positive than those who had layers of shame connected with their math experiences. Not being good at math seems harmless, but often students would tell me they had wanted to pursue a particular field of study but didn't want to take the required math classes. For some, the fear of not graduating because they would be unable to pass math was debilitating.

If beliefs about math affect life decisions, how much more so the belief that I was the very cause of my own abuse? The internalized message that my trauma was the result of who I had been since I was little lived with me always. To live life, though, this message had to be buried in a part of me so deep it never saw the light of day. When we finally got there, it came out of me as an indescribable explosion of darkness.

Full healing was never possible until this false message was unearthed. Yes, God helped me rise above the pain and gave me strength to live my life. But as a survivor without help to heal, abundance was right outside of my reach. Only complete healing of the core messages I accepted as a child brought true healing. Some of us know the messages and merely need help to heal them. My messages were buried so completely, it took two years of intensive therapy to find all of them. Jeannie did an astounding job of concealing them. To truly heal, it was necessary to go deep.

STEP 4: NEVER LOSE YOUR SENSE OF HUMOR

There were many hours of despair, but I was gifted with the ability to see humor in almost anything. During every session, there was some point where Dr. Sue and I shared laughter. While my humor had sometimes been used as a defense mechanism, laughter was my only true access to joy. I described it as "when I most feel whole and healthy." No matter how deep the distress, I could always manage to laugh and it often showed up in my writing. This is one of the examples I found in my copious files.

The Truth about Giraffes and Therapy (Spring 2016)

With the words to a song about climbing out of the rubble drifting through my head, I entered the giraffe building at our local zoo. It had been a long year, and it was a nice break to go on an adventure with a friend. After this visit to the zoo, I was going to what we all hoped was my final therapy session. I was confident and had my notes ready.

Stepping into the ill-lit building, I found myself tripping over something. Arms flailing wildly, and struggling to gain my balance, I slowly got my feet to stop tripping over whatever was under me and stood still.

My friend asked, "Are you OK?"

I was. We looked at each other with relief … and then, *Bam!* I was on the ground.

While trying to collect my pride, I heard the nice young man selling lettuce leaves to feed to the giraffes ask, "Ma'am, are you OK?"

I said yes and asked him to help me up.

Looking at my friend, I said, "What was that? I was fine—then I was on the ground. What happened?"

Behind me was a stack of large mats. They had cushioned my fall, but they were also the cause of falling in the first place.

The giraffe over my head looked at me quizzically. His head was tilted exactly like Dr. Sue's each time she had thought I was on my feet only to see me fall flat once again.

"There is another layer. There is something else," she'd say.

This scenario had been repeated again and again; but on this day I was feeling confident as I went to my session and sat on the couch for possibly the last time (hope springs eternal).

"I went to the zoo today."

The look of delight on Dr. Sue's face was rewarding. I had spent a week in bed not long before this, so going to the zoo was certainly a good sign.

"I fell."

"What?"

In telling the story, the parallels between my balancing act, moment of relief, and subsequent fall looked a lot like therapy.

Trip. Flail wildly. Regain balance. "I'm good." Moment of relief. *Bam!* On the floor.

I began laughing and couldn't stop. It was good to hear my laughter in the office, which had been filled with tears for so many months.

Dr. Sue laughed with me. Then she stopped and looked at me. "You held out your hands and asked him to help you up."

We stared at each other as the import of this sank in. I had reached out my hands to a man to help me. This was excellent progress from the awkward day a few weeks earlier when I had refused to shake the hand of the church greeter.

Yes, I fell a lot; but when I got on my feet again, it was always in a better place. It wasn't my last session; but I was back on my feet and so much better!

And the giraffes were impressed.

STEP 5: TAKING FINAL EXAMS

Just when I would think The Curriculum had ended, I would find myself enrolled in another course. There was always a final exam—a culminating experience, which would bring a new level of healing. These finals were never easy, but they helped me understand how far I had come. I wish I had understood the purpose of these final exams better. I would have been less likely to confuse the final exam with graduation. I would have told Dr. Sue I was "done" far less often!

One particular final exam, which was delivered to me at church, was a key part of The Curriculum because I had to apply so much in order to walk through it. It involved abuse, triggers, messages, and feelings. It affected all parts of me, because it spoke to the deeply buried message. No one could help me walk through this painful layer.

Scott and I were waiting for the service to begin. I glanced at the bulletin and saw a familiar song listed. I nudged Scott and pointed.

When he saw what song it was, he sighed and rolled his eyes. "Here we go."

For months, this song had invaded my world. I hadn't heard it for years, but for some reason it had returned in various new forms. There was no question about why it bothered me—why the words sent me to dark places.

When peace like a river, attendeth my way,
When sorrows like sea billows roll;
Whatever my lot, Thou hast taught me to say
It is well, it is well, with my soul.

This beautiful song was written by hymnist Horatio Spafford in the late 1800s after multiple tragedies struck his family. My problem with the song was because I sat in pews and listened to it being sung by some whose souls were anything but "well." I knew this because they had robbed the song from me. It had been several months since my reaction to the song had been identified as a trigger and, at that time, part of me rebelled and began screaming.

"You make me listen to men sing this song when you know they may be lying! You know what happened."

It was Nine. She was right. I walked out and promised to never make her sit through the song again—a promise kept by walking out several more times.

One day, while sitting in the home of a long-time friend, I realized the lyrics to this song had been beautifully framed and hung on the wall behind the couch—just above her head. No, not everyone who sang and loved the song did horrible unspeakable things—certainly not this gentle friend. It really was well with her soul. My innocent self who was betrayed deserved to be honored, but I also needed to remember this song did ring true in the souls of many good people who could be trusted.

The service kept marching toward the song. I had promised my inner child she would never be forced to sit through the song again. The door was directly behind me; it would be easy to leave. But, I wondered, was this just one more thing my abusers had taken from me?

Scott leaned toward me and said, "It's OK if you need to leave."

Yes, it would be OK to leave, but I sensed when the child inside me saw the song above my dear friend's couch she had come to terms with the truth. The song was not meant to be a lie. She seemed to be fine with staying. But someone else wasn't.

"It is my young adult self who needs to have a new memory in this new church where everyone's story is safe."

The week before, I had uncovered the river memory and my mother's message. I understood how my broken spirit tried to live above the pain. My search for help had resulted in weak men taking advantage of my fragile state, causing the message to be internalized in even more damaging ways. Yes, this young adult who became trapped in her pain needed a new message.

"I am going to stay but will need tissues."

"Yes, you will," he said, as he set out to find a tissue box at the back of the room.

When the song began, I was thankful for the volume of the music, the darkness of the room, and the anonymity of being one of a thousand. The pain erupted.

Every tissue was used and as the song was coming to a close, I spoke aloud, "You will not rob me of this song any longer. It was not well with your soul and you damaged mine, but I will never leave again because I cannot listen. You will rob me no longer. I have fought for my soul and now, yes, I can finally say it is well with my soul."

Yes, it is well with my soul. I blamed myself always. But I have spent thousands and gone through box after box of tissue to be able to sing this song. To all who are weak and broken, I say, "Get the help you need. Do not inflict your pain on the innocent who trust you. Do not see their brokenness as opportunity to gratify your own pathetic needs. Never sing this song unless it is true to the depth of your being. This song is mine. I will no longer allow the pain you inflicted to rob me of knowing it is well with my soul."

Yes, they may have sung it as a lie, but I sing it as truth. It's over. My healing has stopped my abuser's lies from controlling me any longer. The cage door is open. I am getting ready to fly.

I looked at Scott. "That was really brave."

"Yes, it was."

He is always a bit amazed at how I grab the tiger of oppression by the tail and swing with all my might. We had both watched this one fly out of the room and land in the rubbish heap of pain and suffering.

FINAL THOUGHTS ON THE CURRICULUM

As I reflect back on all that The Curriculum taught me, I feel as though I have completed a second Ph.D.—this time on myself. Much of what I came to believe about children was confirmed, but my understanding of the ways in which insecure attachment and early childhood trauma affect a child's development and adult mental health was changed and expanded in ways that are almost incomprehensible. My understanding of myself, and the turmoil I lived above my entire life, makes what I accomplished fall into the category of "miraculous."

Probably the most astounding realization is how the human mind is capable of repressing memories of trauma. Without The Curriculum, all of my cover stories would have remained intact and prevented me from healing. Repression was key to survival, but it also prevented me from ever processing trauma. Only God and I knew the whole story, and I had to remember it in manageable pieces—and in the order that would make sense to me. This is what The Curriculum accomplished.

My journey has made me alert to the fact that, even outside of my healing process, God is attempting to communicate with me every moment of every single day. The Curriculum is not just for healing—it is an invitation to a relationship. Much like an invitation to a dance, we can turn away, watch but not participate, or we can get out on the floor and dance.

For months on end, the song "Shut up and Dance" would play at times when I needed it most—in malls, at church (yes), in my car, etc. One line in the song says, "This woman is my destiny." I never doubted but God was speaking to me through this song, telling me to continue to accept his invitation into the dance of relationship and healing—and reminding me to never stop trusting Dr. Sue.

Ah, The Curriculum. It never ceases to surprise and delight me. It is a dance with God.

20
Writing My Future

Early in therapy, Dr. Sue asked me, "Janyne what do you want to do?"

All the paths in my brain came up with nothing. This had never been seen as a legitimate question. I had thought better questions would be, "What do you need to do?" or "What are you called to do?"

To all these questions, I now say, "Write!"

I have included in these pages only a fraction of what I wrote during my journey. Writing helped me to heal, and healing allowed me to finally do what I had always wanted to do—write. Writing also enabled me to clarify my goals and choices. The decision to tell my story in public ways, including blogging and writing this book, involved over a year of soul searching and healing. This journey is embedded in the pieces below. You will see how the writing process convinced me to tell my story and spend the remainder of my days writing about the life I had been freed to live.

SITTING ON THE BAY (FEBRUARY 2016)

The bench at the edge of a causeway called me to sit and rest. It was a beautiful February day in San Diego. The sky was perfectly clear, and the breeze was pleasant. How unexpected, to find myself in one of my favorite cities on such a beautiful day.

There are two directions boats could take from the causeway. One led to a cozy harbor; the other led to the ocean. One was safe and predictable with few waves. The other would be an unknown adventure. It felt like my life. God really didn't care which path was chosen. This was a new concept for me. God wanted to heal me so I could make my own choices? It was *my* choice?

I had to figure out who that small child really wanted to be—before she had to become what everyone else wanted her to be. Was she cautious by choice? I think not. The One Who Lived really knew no fear. She was conditioned to be fearful and hypervigilant. The child selves inside of me were doing so much better. Their life had been difficult and I had no desire to plunge them into waves that would bring more damage. We could live quietly and enjoy a simple life. We could find peace and be happy. Maybe we could do this?

Out of the corner of my eye, a tour boat passed by as it headed to the ocean. The tour guide spoke excitedly. "It is a beautiful sunny day, and I am looking forward to getting out on the ocean and finding some seals and whales!"

The explorer in me stirred. Yes, the cove would be safe and predictable, but it is not where adventure happens. Yet, it was peaceful there and the waves wouldn't reach me. If that is what I wanted, it was there for me to have, but would I be content to merely watch the tour boat head out to sea every day? Did I need to feel safe, or did I merely desire peace? Peace was not a bad idea.

God was neither choosing nor telling me what to do. It was my decision. The abundant life could be found in either place. Both choices would pose challenges and advantages. It was my choice to make.

This was huge and completely overwhelming.

TO WRITE OR NOT TO WRITE: THAT IS THE QUESTION (FEBRUARY 2017)

Up and ready to begin my day, I found myself hesitant to start. With an entire day to write, it seemed like an opportunity that should not be squandered. Especially since there was a deadline! Self-imposed, but a deadline all the same. A decision deadline, which was both motivating and slowing me down.

It was a rather existential deadline, since it had everything to do with the meaning of my life. I wrote,

> I am not who I was, nor do I think I am who I will be, but on this day I can only be who I am. Who is that, I wonder? I wish it were simpler than it appears in this particular moment.

I remember that day. I remember feeling like I was living life in limbo.

"Let's see, I am not who I used to be—a very tightly controlled image of perfection who was always a tad frayed around the edges and ready to divert with self-deprecating humor. Ah, the inner pain and turmoil the perfection hid! No, thankfully, I am not who I was. Phew. Healing was a two-year tumble into humanness."

Yes, Alice had fallen down the rabbit hole in her head. Just as in the story of Alice, I emerged from the rabbit hole a much different person. Yet on the day in question, I was far from there. I wrote:

> I don't think I am who I am to become—but becoming is so dependent on choices. My book is finished and the tedious editing, slashing, rethinking, and revising processes

are in motion. My story is a gift to myself. My website is re-purposed and ready to launch, now that I actually know what I want to say. Yes, the process is marching forward.

Some months later, it was still true that the only thing I lacked was for my soul to get on board the swiftly moving book express. I was standing at the platform and the train was in the station. The door of limitless possibilities was open and my future was right on the other side. What was holding me back?

What held me back is the understanding that this choice would in some ways determine my future. Not that I couldn't make choices as I went along, but the choice to tell my story would determine the general direction of my life.

Behind me stood a crowd who had come to cheer me on. Some, like those in my writing class alumni group, knew exactly what I planned to say. Others kind of knew. Still others were clueless and were just cheering the "me" they thought me to be. Then there were my children—all grown and living their own lives. They were cheering simply because I was Mom, but after stepping on board the train, my story would be part of our future as a family. I can't help but consider them—and the grandchildren.

No, this decision couldn't be made on the basis of the cheering crowd. It was an existential problem only I could decide. Probably only two people understood the soul searching—my husband and Dr. Sue—but they couldn't decide for me. It was my choice.

The question was: Could there be meaning to my life outside of stepping onboard the book express? Absolutely, but once on board, there was no stopping the train. I could run to the front of the train and decide where it should go—maybe, but no emergency brake existed. There was no saying, "Oh, that wasn't a good idea; I should get off now."

So I had to be sure. It was important to look inside my soul to see if there was any other choice. On the days when a choice was evident, it wasn't really very appealing. It involved hiding and hoping someone didn't tell my story without my permission. It involved fear and living in the cage of my former self. It involved watching others live in their pain and never giving them the hope for healing that I had to offer. It involved hearing discussions about mental health and never adding to the conversation. It involved allowing ignorance to have a voice but silencing my own.

Well, when put that way, it wasn't really a choice, was it? It seemed there was not really much of value I would lose by getting on board—but there was so much potential loss by standing on the platform for the remainder of my life.

Back to the existential question. Could there be meaning to my life outside of stepping onboard the book express? I am more than my story, and my life is more than my story. So, yes, I could continue to heal and find meaning in a life filled with quiet pursuits, family, and friends.

Out of the corner of my eye, I saw Jeannie—my small child self. She was composed of so many parts of me: my warrior, my explorer, my problem solver, my writer, my comforter, and so much more. She was opinionated and strong. She was resilient and tenacious. She had her hands on her hips and she was glaring at my indecision. She fought to save my life and now she wanted me to live it—freely.

I held out my hand to her. I was feeling old and tired from my journey. I was not completely healed. I needed her. I needed to remember who I was inside—at my core. The train was starting to pull out. She grabbed my hand, and we began to run. We both laughed as we leapt onto the train and rolled across the floor in a tangled heap.

"Are you OK?" I asked her.

She laughed. "Of course I am. You are the old one."

"You are right! But you help me feel young again. Thank you for helping me catch the train."

And with an impish look, she said, "You're very welcome, but we need to get up there and take control of where this train is headed."

I watched her begin to run toward the front of the train. She was always in the yellow dress, and her chin was always set in determination. What could possibly be any more meaningful than being on an adventure with this child inside of me? What could be any more important than helping her live out the life she was meant to live? What would she do? I wondered. What did she want to tell the world? Where did she intend for the train to go? What absolutely delightful surprises did she have in store for me?

Hefting my body off the floor, I thought, "I better get back in shape if I intend to keep up with this one!"

Running after the child "me" in the yellow dress, the train lurched, and we both laughed as I stumbled and then caught up with her. She grabbed my hand, and we were off!

The decision was made, and the book needed to be ready before the train took the next turn. Jeannie and I had our hands on the controls, and we were headed to our future—together.

A Possible Ending

If you are reading this sentence, it is proof of my freedom. I have written my way to freedom. Fear tried to take me prisoner, but I said, "No, you will not hold me captive."

I put my fingers on the keyboard of my life; and God, Scott, Dr. Sue, and all twenty-plus parts of me unlocked the cage of my abusers and set me free.

It is hard to conclude a story while still living but harder to write it once dead. It is truly a conundrum. We have made it here to this conclusion of sorts, and it seems appropriate to end with pieces that best reflect the struggle, the triumph, the search for meaning, and ultimately answered the question Dr. Sue asked me:

"Janyne, what do you want to do?"

Jeannie and Janyne always wanted to live. Every structure, repressed memory, cover story, and dissociative strategy was designed for that purpose.

I want to live life.

And with that, my healed self climbed on Jeannie's bike to fly over the rainbow with the bluebirds. There were new worlds to explore. Scott found his long-forgotten bike and pedaled after me with anticipation for what we would do together. We had survived a mental-health and life tsunami and were on our way. We smiled knowing we had never given up on each other.

Pausing to wave back to Dr. Sue, I said, "Thank you for helping my troubles melt like lemon drops. You will be with me wherever I go. Our story will never end because healing lasts forever—generation after generation. Everyone I help will be because of what you did for me. I will be back to tell you about my adventures—and if I ever need help, I promise to ask."

She smiled and waved.

As we pedaled out of sight, I heard God say, "Well done."

Epilogue

Therapy had ended, but I was staring at walls again. My blogs were being read. My book was done. My life was moving forward. So many life complications had been solved. It seemed we would be staying in Colorado longer than expected. I was both sad and relieved by this, but having ambivalent emotions was beginning to make more sense. It seemed it was what it was supposed to be. Yet, I was staring at walls.

It wasn't that there weren't things I wanted to do, I just couldn't do them. As soon as I began, something (someone) stopped me. Then I knew. She was four. She was the child who wandered through the house trapped in her own home where the attention she needed simply could not be found. It only took one simple question while having a glass of iced tea with a friend on a very hot day for this four-year-old child to explode into the conversation. I contacted Dr. Sue and made an appointment.

Needing help again was disconcerting but necessary. If I was to ever accomplish what I knew was set before me, I somehow had to find out why this small child stopped me from continuing. I wasn't even sure how my friend and I had caused her to step forward over tea. Could I find her again? I thought I had to go back and wander in the house with her again, but instead she took me to church.

There were so many who loved me at church, but I felt myself being dragged away from them as they complimented me. I felt myself engaging with them, but becoming fearful as my mother entered the room. I felt myself being dragged away again and again. Then I saw him. He had known me from the time I was a baby. He always had candy for me. "Hello, Jeannie, it looks like you have new shoes on today." I loved shoes. I grinned at him and looked down at my shoes as he handed me my candy. Then she was there pulling me away. I felt the shame wash over me. I wasn't supposed to try to get attention.

Then I heard my mother talking. The darkness swam around me. She was telling me to stop trying to get attention. She asked, "Do you remember what happened to you?" I did. I didn't want to, but I did. "Do you want that to happen to you again?" I shook my head no. I never wanted that to happen again. "Then you need to stop trying to get attention."

I opened my eyes but couldn't look at Dr. Sue. Was that why I had come back to therapy, to get attention? Was that why I was blogging? Was that why I was telling my story? I tried to express this, and I could hear her voice reaching across my thoughts. "Janyne, what are the reasons for blogging and writing your book?"

Suddenly back to my adult self, I said, "Because I want to help people. I want to help children. I want to help adults understand children."

Then I understood. This part of me was afraid that the attention I would receive was going to cause me to be hurt. She thought I was doing this to get attention. I looked at Dr. Sue, "I am not doing it for attention, am I?"

She laughed and said with a smile, "No, Janyne, you aren't trying to get attention, you are trying to help people."

I suddenly felt both four and sixty four at the same time. There was something that I had felt in the memory.

"Deep in the memory, I felt something else. It was an understanding that my mother was trying to protect me."

Dr. Sue and I stared at each other and understood the significance of this realization. We came back to it twice and the second time, I realized that my thinking was changing. She was a really lousy mother in so many ways; but whatever had happened to her as a child, consciously or unconsciously caused her to try to stop my attention-seeking behaviors so I would not be abused again.

"She didn't even understand she was the cause of the behaviors. I think she blamed herself for whatever happened to her as a child and projected it on me. Her mother was always ill, her father was a mean man, and she had needed attention as much as I did."

We will never know what happened to her, but everything we had found indicated that my abuse had triggered memories and caused her to project her pain onto me. I understood how difficult it was to control those painful reenactments of my own childhood. She was unable to do so.

The tears poured down my face. I was so sad for the small child who believed her abuse was caused by her own attention-seeking behaviors. I was sad for my mother's inability to give the attention that would have stopped the cycle. It was a cycle that would repeat itself again and again in my life. She never knew me. She missed so much.

"I have forgiven her."

Dr. Sue looked both startled and amazed. "Does this feel true?"

Yes, it did.

"You are well, Janyne. You can forgive because you have healed."

I grinned. She was right. Forgiveness happens when healing is finished. The grief was over. The anger was over. The need to understand was over. It didn't change all the really awful things she said and did, but I didn't have to carry it around anymore. I was simply sad that my mother was too broken to ever know me. This side of eternity, she would never understand why I am doing what I am doing, but I believe on the other side, she knows, understands, and is glad I inherited her tenacious spirit so I can help others heal and break the generational patterns that destroy relationships between mothers and their children.

Some months later, while completing the last edits and changes in this book, I came to the conclusion that the right thing to do was to dedicate the book to my mother. Scott was surprised. Dr. Sue was surprised. My publisher was surprised. Most of all, I was surprised. It was stunning evidence of healing of the very deepest kind. I could never change my mother's brokenness, but I did understand that she never intended to inflict so much damage. In her own brokenness she could never meet my needs.

I know why I chose to be brave. I chose to be brave for every person who needed to believe in healing, but also for every mother who truly desires to know and love her children.

ADDENDUM
Childhood Trauma

One sunny but cold February day, I sat down to try to address the emotions underlying the children's stories. With Scott away on a business trip, I had dedicated the time to finally facing my greatest fear—the emotions of a small child. We had worked through hundreds of layers to get to this point. Some of those layers occurred during my pre-teen, teen, and young adult years. Everything that occurred after the initial abuse at three was rooted in the emotions of this small child and her attempts to live life despite the pain she held inside.

What I had come to realize was my greatest fear was the emotional chaos of a small child trying to make sense of what she was completely incapable of understanding. It was the dark cloud I had run from my entire life. It had overtaken me the day, as a three year old, I sat abandoned on the floor in the corner of my room. If it is possible for a small child to experience hell, that is what I felt. I have wanted to cry every single day of my life since then; but it was oh, so important not to cry.

So, on that cold February day, I decided to explain how a small child who has been sexually abused feels—and to let myself cry. These are the tragic threads of what we uncovered in the tangled web of my three-year-old mind and what I would have needed in order to not live out the results of it for my entire life.

During the 1950s an understanding of trauma was almost nonexistent. My parents could not understand the damage that was occurring in my mind and body. Today, with appropriate interventions, we are able to help abused children heal. This cannot happen, though, unless we break the silence that surrounds sexual abuse.

THE NEED FOR ATTACHMENT

Insecure attachment was the precursor to the abuse. My father, brother, and church family did the best they could to meet the emotional needs my mother was unable to provide. I did not lack attention. But in the most important relationship for a young child—that of a mother—I was left with a vacuum. This resulted in my need to look elsewhere for attention. When this happens to a child, he or she becomes a prime target for a predator. I trusted the man in the day care. He played blocks with me.

What my small self needed: Attention. A mother's love. I needed someone to say, "You did nothing wrong to want attention and to trust him. What he did to you was wrong. You didn't do anything wrong."

BETRAYAL

The abuse embedded trust issues into my psyche. My abuser was a person in a position of trust, and he betrayed me, but my need for attachment would lead me into similar situations again and again. The emotional need for attachment would always override my fear of trusting. This emotional war between mistrust and insecure attachment played out in therapy in multiple ways. My need to trust in order to survive while mistrusting everyone was a psychological battle of immense proportions. As a three year old, my mind simply froze in fear because the one I trusted to give me attention was the one who hurt me. I cannot even imagine the pain and confusion for children abused through incest. My father's care for me provided a stronghold in my life.

What my small self needed: Assurance I would never have to go back there and I would be protected. I needed to have it explained to me. I needed to feel safe. I also needed help in understanding who could be trusted.

To Be Believed

The abuse occurred the second time because I was not believed. I didn't have words to explain, but my emotional trauma was evident. I am sure every person in the building heard me during the therapy session when the memory of not wanting to return to the daycare surfaced. I cried and screamed and felt myself flailing in protest. The processing left me completely shaken. I understand my parents needed to move on with their day, and it might have appeared like a temper tantrum, but even that would have a cause. This was beyond a temper tantrum. I needed someone to listen.

Toward the end of therapy, the reality surfaced of my childhood nightmares, in which I had relived the trauma over and over. My dad would sit beside me, trying to comfort me back to sleep, telling me it was only a dream. He was doing his very best to comfort me, but because no one ever talked about what happened to me, I was unintentionally being told my memory was only a dream.

The lack of conversation around what happened caused me to think what had happened to me was somehow "normal." The abuse became part of my childhood just like going to school. It might not always be pleasant, but it was just part of being a little girl. No one wanted me to talk about it, so I just accepted it. Later, when I understood the abuse was wrong, my mind had already learned to dissociate, repress, and move on.

What my small self needed: Talking about the abuse would have prevented many psychological problems. During the 1950s no one knew this. It was believed I would forget. But the body never forgets. The dreams were an indicator that my little mind was trying to process the trauma. Children's night terrors need to be taken seriously. Even when abuse is not involved, it is an indicator that their little minds need help in processing fear. What I needed was a compassionate voice to say, "It was terrible what happened to you. You can talk about it. You can cry. You are safe now. I will protect you. And if it ever happens again, you can tell us."

To Be the Child and Cry

Tragically, it was necessary for my small self to take on the responsibility of not troubling my mother by crying. My dad needed me to be brave. He was caught between caring for the woman he loved and the small girl he adored. I never fully understood the bond we shared until I processed his care for me in the days following the abuse. He was protecting me, and I was protecting him—by not crying and causing distress in our home. I sucked on my fingers, I held my puppy, and I was forced to learn how to control myself. My subconscious protected me by repressing the memory and eventually causing me to split into parts so I could contain the pain.

My first split was based on this need to separate my need to cry from my life. This inability to stop myself from crying, despite desperate control measures to keep it from happening, followed me throughout life. My hatred for Jane and fear of my feelings were part of this fear of crying. I also made many decisions along the way that were bound in the need to be the adult and not bother my mother and thereby protect my father. This would have heartbreaking results during my early teen and young adult years.

What my small self needed: To cry. To be held. To release the trauma and pain. I needed to be a child. I needed my mother to be the adult. I needed someone to say, "Cry, Jeannie, cry. Cry until you don't need to cry anymore."

Connections and Triggers

Every child makes incorrect connections and conclusions. When these are somehow connected to the emotional trauma of abuse, they become irrational triggers. The triggers resulting from my abuse were always seemingly unrelated. Some of those are explained in this book, but the one which most affected me from the time I was three was always tied to "my turn is coming." Without my absolute determination to live my life above the pain, this one could have been professionally debilitating. As a child, it overtook me most often when having to run relays or coming to the front of the line at cafeterias. The anxiety involved in these situations was indescribable. I was not born an anxious child; my anxiety had a cause.

The faulty connections were numerous. How could chain link fences and bunk beds be connected? It makes no sense, but they were. These were not debilitating but followed me always. The chain link fence connection was clearly from the house where the abuse occurred, but I would need to go stay with friends and sleep in a bunk bed for five nights for the connection to surface. Bunk beds were connected to the days after the abuse when I was reliving the trauma in my dreams. I remember going to camp as a child/teen and obsessing over getting a top bunk for weeks before I arrived. Add my difficulty with having my feet trapped in sleeping bags (e.g., trapped in the hospital blanket I was brought back home in) and I am sure I appeared quite dogmatic and possibly odd. These connections were relatively innocuous.

But the connections between physical (pleasurable) responses to abuse and the ensuing pain and resulting shame are far reaching. For a young child to experience sensations beyond her understanding is confusing and has tragic effects. The hot wash of shame flowed out of me for two years in wrenching sobs and piles of tissues. The dark cloud was shame. The tangled, confused thoughts inside my young mind were bound by shame. The shame would eventually tell me to cut up Jane and throw her over a cliff. My irrational hatred of my own being grew out of the desperately dark thoughts of an abused three-year-old child who was building connections in her brain that would last a lifetime.

What my small self needed: To be held and told it wasn't wrong for my body to sometimes have feelings that felt good. When I tried to make these feelings happen again by rocking, I needed to be distracted without shame. I needed someone to understand I was trying to soothe myself from the trauma inside of me. I needed to be hugged and comforted so it didn't feel necessary.

The abuse wired me in ways small children should not be wired, and this needed to be accepted. My greatest need was to be soothed; but without the hugs and holding I needed, I resorted to what had felt good. I needed to not feel everything I did to try to help myself was shameful. I needed to be helped in finding alternatives for soothing myself and not shamed for using the only ones available to me.

In fact, it seemed there was nothing that wasn't shameful when it came to my needs. To seek attention was shameful. My trust for my perpetrator was shameful. Allowing him to touch me was shameful. Throwing a tantrum to protect myself was shameful. Screaming at my mother when she rejected me was shameful. My crying was shameful. My throwing up from the trauma was shameful. My body was dirty and shameful. Sucking on my fingers was shameful. But the very worst was the shame of how I helped my body soothe.

I Couldn't Play

Because I believed that my betrayal resulted from playing blocks with my abuser, playing was laden with feelings of betrayal. The message that bad things happen when you are having fun followed me always. I never understood the deep feeling that enjoying my life was a precursor to pain and betrayal. In addition, I now understand I was suffering from early childhood depression that affected my brain development. This set a lifetime struggle with depression in motion and would finally make it necessary to use antidepressants for much of my adult life.

I actually taught the importance of play at multiple in-service opportunities over the years. I knew play was as natural to a child as breathing, but I also knew I could not play, not really. There were exceptions to this, but for the most part it was true. I could set up play experiences for my children or children in my classroom, but I was unable to enter in. Over the years, I brought many college students into my home to play with my children. I have been learning to play with my granddaughter, but it is a long journey.

I created inner children who did play. I loved hopscotch, jacks, jump rope, and foursquare. No one would have known a part of me was standing back and watching but never playing. I lived my life that way. I took pictures to enjoy later, but I was never completely there.

What my small self needed: Someone to notice I wasn't playing. I needed someone to bring me next to them and show me how to play again. I simply could not bring myself to fully enter into the experience. I needed someone to take my hand and bring me into the playing. What should have come naturally had been severely damaged and needed to be rekindled.

My Fear of Feelings

I hated my feelings, because they were so dark and there was no way to resolve or deal with them. I couldn't work through sadness, because I would need to cry. I couldn't work through anger, because it was explosive and mixed with fear. I couldn't even accept love, because it required trust, and my trust had been betrayed. My fear could not be resolved, because I never understood I would not be sent back. The stress and pain of unresolved feelings was building inside of me. I was doing my best to cope, but I was only small.

There have been so many times in my life when I was emotionally three and I would suddenly find myself entangled in a web of irrational fears and thoughts. Sometimes I screamed. It was probably the very primal scream of isolation and rejection that exploded out of me as hatred of my mother. Betrayal was the most likely instigator of the primal scream, but fear of rejection was right alongside it. Sometimes I threw myself face first on the floor. It was difficult to explain.

I spent my life hiding the small three-year-old self who lived in her own personal hell deep inside my body. I held her there with all the control I could muster. I told cover stories around my other abuse experiences, but my greatest fear was the exposure of the darkest and deepest fear embedded inside the body of the three year old. She held the feelings I would never be able to control should they escape. I left her there when I began to split.

Feelings were not what I feared. I feared the three-year-old child inside of me. I was not rejecting feelings per se. I was rejecting the emotional turmoil of my child self and her inability to process. She was the shameful part of me who could not control herself. She was the one who was needy and brought the abuse. She was the one who plunged me into despair. I always saw adult Jane holding her, but in reality she was inside each one I created to hold pain. She was the one who cried in the bed. She was the one who sealed up memories. She was the one who lived in the basement of shame. She was the one who held the stories. She was the one who learned how to comfort us. All of the splits were my way of separating myself from her—from my feelings that never felt like anything but the emotional turmoil of a small abused child.

What my small self needed: Help understanding my emotions. This would have required talking through them. My young mind registered everything as trauma. Even good surprises could potentially create fear ("Never throw a surprise party for me," I told Scott). When I reacted in oddly incorrect ways, I needed help in understanding why. To do this, it would have been necessary to talk to me about the abuse and watch my reactions carefully in order to break unnecessary connections before they became phobias. This would have required others to acknowledge and accept my feelings as valid and understandable.

To Sum It Up

The bottom line is I needed hugs (which I may have seemed not to want). I needed a safe place to cry. I needed my feelings to be acknowledged. I needed help in understanding what happened to me was not my fault. I needed help in processing those connections that were made as a result of abuse, so I could be free from them. I needed to learn ways to care for myself, to calm myself, to be kind to myself. I needed someone to help me remember who I was before the abuse—the child I was created to be. I needed to know there was nothing bad about me. I wasn't bad: something bad happened to me.

Yes, I needed all those things; but instead, I waited sixty years and sat on a therapist's couch for hundreds of hours. In God's wisdom, I was sent to a therapist who did understand and was willing to care for me in all the ways I needed as a small child. She worked tirelessly to help heal and care for each fragmented child inside of me while helping my integrated adult self understand how to be the mother they never had. I slept with my puppy, threw sticks in the stream, and so much more to learn how to help these small children feel safe. I learned that, with the right help, I could have healed. The final tragic chapters of my abuse did not have to happen. My father did the best he could with limited understanding and lots of love, but I also needed a mother who loved me, hugged me while I cried, and delighted in me. I found this in therapy and have now learned to care for myself in the ways my mother never could. We can all do this for the children in our lives that have experienced traumas both big and small. Every child needs to be fully seen and accepted.

ACKNOWLEDGMENTS

My deepest gratitude to:

• My husband, Scott, who was my steady rock during this journey. No words can explain the mountains we climbed, the exhaustion we felt, or the decisions we had to make. We both fought for each other, but he was my protector every single day. Together we demonstrated the depth of commitment and love required to come out on the other side of a mental health and life tsunami.

• My therapist, Dr. Susan Kwiecien, who always believed I could heal and worked tirelessly to make it true. Her care for me (and all the children inside of me) will never be forgotten. Her professionalism, dedication, and skill will live on in every moment I embrace and each word I write.

• Jeannie Ann, my child self who was composed of many fractured parts, and fought to live my life. To all those I called Jane and Janyne, the ones who held the pain and the ones who lived, and Non Janyne who enabled me to live my adult life. To each one I owe a debt of gratitude.

• My adult children who love me as Mom and support my desire to help others with my story. Their lives give me hope that generational patterns can be broken.

• My dad, Kenneth Jenkins, who loved me and called me Jeannie Ann with a smile of delight until he left this world at the age of one hundred. His kind and gentle spirit lives on in me.

• My brothers, Lee and Richard Jenkins who supported me and helped me walk through our family memories in ways that promoted healing and allowed me to tell our story.

- My friends and relatives who both believed me and believed in me. They could never fully understand, but their listening ears, words of encouragement, and prayers provided the safety I needed to heal. There are too many to name, but of special note are those who lived here in Colorado Springs and were able to support me through my struggles and triumphs with hugs, lunches, and cups of coffee!

- The growing network of supporters, including fellow writers from my writing class, therapists, Healing States 365, the Attachment and Trauma Network (ATN), author Thomas J. Oord and those involved in the Uncontrolling Love of God network, Discovery Church Colorado, and my Janyne.org blog followers. Thank you to all who have helped me to believe my words could provide hope for healing.

- Both my first editor, Lisa Michaels, and my publisher, Cathy Lawton, who believed in the importance of telling my story.

- The Garden of the Gods RV Resort where we came to heal and rebuild our lives and found community and acceptance. The employees, "full-timers," work campers and guests, all helped me to slowly begin my life again with smiles, hugs, yoga, and workouts at the gym.

- Tom and Glee Mahon who enabled us to buy their fifth wheel and drove it across the country to us. This life and our future would not have been possible without their help. We live the blessing they prayed over our new home and life every single day. They truly delivered our future.

- Last, but not least, God, who led me to Dr. Sue (the embodiment of every caring act I had ever given others). I stand in awe of "The Curriculum" and the ways our needs were met in truly amazing and unexpected ways.

Janyne McConnaughey, Ph.D., retired from a forty-year career in education in order to heal from the effects of the childhood abuse she had suffered. During therapy she wrote her way to healing and now is redeeming her story by helping others to understand and heal from childhood trauma.

Along with *Brave: A Personal Story of Healing Childhood Trauma*, Janyne is working on two forthcoming sequels to this book. She also keeps busy blogging at Janyne.org, and guest blogging for other organizations addressing childhood trauma.

Janyne enjoys full-time RV living with her husband Scott at the edge of Garden of the Gods in Colorado Springs, Colorado, and treasures the time she spends in the Seattle area with her children and grandchildren.

Find Janyne online:

Website: http://Janyne.org
Twitter: @janynetweets
Facebook: http://www.facebook.com/janynemc/

Made in the USA
Coppell, TX
18 September 2023

21716834R00144